diabetic LIVING®

quick & easy meals

Houghton Mifflin Harcourt
Boston   New York

Copyright © 2011 by Meredith Corporation, Des Moines, IA. All rights reserved

Published by Houghton Mifflin Harcourt Publishing Company

www.hmhco.com

Library of Congress Cataloging-in-Publication Data is available on request
ISBN 978-0-470-87280-2

Printed in China
SCP 10 9 8 7 6 5
4500634246

Meredith Corporation

Editorial Director: Gregory H. Kayko
Special Interest Media

Diabetic Living® Quick and Easy Meals

Food Editor: Jessie Shafer, RD

Art Director: Michelle Bilyeu

Project Editor: Stephanie Karpinske

Cover Photographer: Blaine Moats

Cover Food Stylist: Greg Luna

Houghton Mifflin Harcourt

Publisher: Natalie Chapman

Associate Publisher: Jessica Goodman

Executive Editor: Anne Ficklen

Editor: Adam Kowit

Editorial Assistant: Cecily McAndrews

Production Director: Diana Cisek

Senior Production Editor: Amy Zarkos

Cover Design: Suzanne Sunwoo

Interior Design: Kathryn Finney

Interior Layout: Holly Wittenberg

Graphics/Imaging: Brent Savage

Manufacturing Manager: Tom Hyland

Our seal assures you that every recipe in *Diabetic Living Quick & Easy Meals* has been tested in the Better Homes and Gardens® Test Kitchen. This means that each recipe is practical and reliable and meets our high standards of taste appeal. We guarantee your satisfaction with this book for as long as you own it.

Fast, delicious, and diabetes friendly? You got it!

After a typically busy day, all you want is a short and simple dinner recipe. One that uses ingredients you already have on hand, fits in your diabetes meal plan, and tastes so delicious that everyone says, "Yum!"

Is that too much to ask? Absolutely not! This cookbook has recipes that fit all those criteria. In fact, most of them are ready to eat in less than 30 minutes. You'll find main dishes for busy weeknights, side dishes you can make in minutes, and super-simple snacks. All of the recipes fit our dietitian-approved nutritional guidelines and have been tested by the Better Homes and Gardens® Test Kitchen.

If you're a *Diabetic Living* magazine reader, you know that we like to give you helpful information to manage diabetes as well as recipes, so we've done that here, too. This book is loaded with tips for making your meals and snacks faster, easier, and more nutritious. Plus, experts from the magazine answer common reader questions, such as which sugar substitutes are best for baking. And if you're newly diagnosed or simply need a quick refresher, check out the first chapter, which provides the basics on eating well to thrive with diabetes.

Whether you're racing home from work, hurrying to get to exercise class, or just want to spend a little less time in the kitchen, we think you'll find that this cookbook offers you the meal solutions you need. We hope you find it a great resource to turn to again and again.

Turn to page 106 to make this delicious spiced beef and mango meal tonight. It can be on your table in less than half an hour!

From the editors of *Diabetic Living*

DiabeticLivingOnline.com

contents

your diabetes
eating plan:

what to know

about counting carbs

Understanding how much carbohydrate you eat and targeting your
individual guidelines are not the only keys to controlling your diabetes.

A diagnosis of diabetes means keeping track of what and how much you eat, specifically when it comes to carbohydrate. Counting carbohydrate, or carbs for short, is a common approach to diabetes meal planning because research shows carbohydrate has the greatest impact on blood glucose. After eating any food containing carbohydrate, it breaks down into glucose and enters the bloodstream. This is why your blood glucose rises after eating carbs.

As you start counting carbs, you may think that it's best just to avoid foods that have carbs. But it's important to remember that carbs aren't bad for you. Carbohydrate is the body's main source of fuel, and you need foods with carbohydrate to function. That doesn't mean you have to follow a strict diet of the same foods every day. As long as you eat the amount of carbs that fit in your meal plan, you can enjoy a variety of foods.

Two Types of Carb Counting

Carb counting includes basic and advanced methods. Everyone starts with basic carb counting, no matter how long they've had diabetes. With basic carb counting, you try to eat the same amount of carbohydrate at the same time each day. For example, if you eat 4 carb choices, or 60 grams of carbohydrate, for breakfast, you should aim to eat that amount at breakfast every day. Basic carb counting is often recommended at diagnosis for people who have type 2 diabetes.

What's my number?

Everyone needs different amounts of carbohydrate, depending on factors such as height, weight, age, activity levels, medications, and weight-loss goals. While everyone is different, the guidelines in the chart below are a great place to start. For a personalized meal plan, talk with a registered dietitian.

The ranges below are based on a three-meals-per-day plan. If you feel like you need a snack between meals, choose one that has less than 7–10 grams of carbohydrate per serving or save a carbohydrate serving from one of your meals to enjoy as a snack.

If you are . . .	The recommended carb range is:*
A woman who wants to maintain weight	45–60 g carbs per meal (3–4 carb choices per meal)
A man who wants to maintain weight	60–75 g carbs per meal (4–5 carb choices per meal)
A woman who wants to lose weight	30–55 g carbs per meal (2–3.5 carb choices per meal)
A man who wants to lose weight	50–65 g carbs per meal (3–4 carb choices per meal)
An active woman	56–75 g carbs per meal (4–5 carb choices per meal)
An active man	65–90 g carbs per meal (4–6 carb choices per meal)

*Carbohydrate ranges were recommended by *Type 2 Diabetes Basics* (International Diabetes Center, 2004), *Gestational Diabetes Basics* (International Diabetes Center, 2005), and Donna Kernodle, R.D., M.P.H., CDE with the Diabetes Care Center at Wake Forest University's Baptist Medical Center.

1 carb choice = 15g carb.

Get moving

Staying active is another way you can manage your blood glucose levels. Consistent moderate-intensity exercise helps your cells respond better to insulin. With a better insulin response, your cells use glucose from your blood more efficiently, so glucose readings are lower. Exercise also helps you lose body fat, which can improve insulin sensitivity.

Advanced carb counting, as the name suggests, is a more detailed way of counting carbohydrate that helps people who take insulin several times a day (with multiple daily injections or a pump). It works by matching mealtime insulin doses to the amount of carbohydrate you eat. "Advanced carb counting is the closest we can get to mimicking what the body would do on its own if it could," says Linda Yerardi, M.S., R.D., LDN, CDE, diabetes consultant in Frederick, Maryland. "You don't have to stay in a certain box and eat 35 carbs at breakfast every day. There are more choices, versatility, and flexibility." Advanced carb counting is a great meal-planning method, but it's not for everyone. Figuring insulin-to-carb ratios and sensitivity factors can be complicated and confusing, so it's best to have a physician overseeing you.

1 carb choice = 15 grams of carbohydrate

Be portion-savvy
Learn to estimate portions by using objects or your own hand.

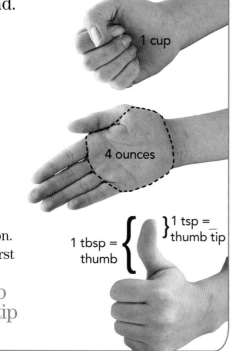

For example:

- A fist equals about 1 cup.
  1 cup = fist

- The palm of an average woman's hand equals about 4 ounces or ½ cup.
  4 ounces = palm

- A thumb is about 1 tablespoon. The tip of the thumb to the first knuckle is about 1 teaspoon.
  1 tablespoon = thumb
  1 teaspoon = thumb tip

Grams or Choices

Carbohydrate is often counted by grams, but some people use choices as well. Your dietitian or certified diabetes educator (CDE) will likely let you choose which method you prefer. When working with carb choices, remember that 1 carb choice is equal to 15 grams of carbohydrate—the amount in one slice of bread or ½ cup cooked pasta.

If you count grams of carbohydrate and aren't familiar with the amount of carbohydrate in foods, you can buy books that list carb content of common foods. Or you can go online to look up the carb content of foods at sites such as the American Diabetes Association's My Food Advisor (http://tracker.diabetes.org/myfoodadvisor.html). This site also lets you type in a recipe so that you can calculate carbs in a casserole, salad, or other mixed dish.

What about exchanges? You may have friends or family members with diabetes who use the Exchange Lists for Meal Planning instead of carb counting. The exchange lists are another way to help you track what you eat. In this plan, food is grouped into six basic types, and the number of servings you need from each food group creates your meal plan. It's simple to use if you eat whole foods that fit into one of the basic food groups but can be confusing if you eat a lot of combination foods, such as soups or casseroles.

Portions Count, Too

Knowing the amount of carbohydrate in a food is important, but you need to stay true to portions as well. If not, you may end up eating three or four times the carbs you thought you were eating. You'll eat more calories as well, which can quickly add on excess pounds. And those extra calories can really add up. An extra handful of potato chips (about ½ cup) can tack 150 calories onto your day. Do it every day and in three months you'll have gained almost 4 pounds from the extra chips alone.

"Weighing and measuring your foods often reveals surprises," says Karmeen Kulkarni, M.S., R.D., BC-ADM, CDE, and co-author of *Complete Guide to Carb Counting* (American Diabetes Association, 2004). "Get out your spoons and scales, dust them off, and keep them on the counter where they stare you down," she says. Use your measuring tools often. When you eyeball a serving, test yourself. Put a portion of rice or cereal on your plate or into your bowl and then transfer it to a measuring cup. Is your estimate correct?

Continue measuring your portions until you're familiar with how they should look. Serving beverages and foods in the same size cups, glasses, bowls, and plates will help. Every few weeks, measure out portions again to make sure you're on track. When you buy fruits and vegetables, pick similar types and sizes. And when buying packaged foods, check labels and count or measure out just one portion.

Track Trends

Keeping detailed food and blood glucose records will help you make the most of counting carbs. "Your tally of carbohydrates each time you eat, coupled with the results from testing your

blood glucose before eating and two hours after, gives you powerful information to spot trends," Kulkarni says.

If your blood glucose is rising too high after eating certain kinds or amounts of foods, try varying your routine, decreasing your carbohydrate intake, or asking if your diabetes medication should be adjusted. Kulkarni suggests working with a diabetes educator who is versed in carb counting to help you adjust your eating plan or exercise or medication routines.

You can find an American Diabetes Association Recognized Education Program in your area by searching diabetes.org/education/edustate2.asp or a registered dietitian by searching "Find a Nutrition Professional" on the American Dietetic Association's Web site, eatright.org.

Keep at It

Counting carbs may seem complicated at first, but the more you do it, the easier it will get. The same is true for estimating portions. Over time, you'll be able to know just what you need in your eating plan in order to manage your glucose levels and feel your best.

guide to
our recipes

See how the Better Homes and Gardens® Test Kitchen calculates nutrition information and helps you count exchanges and carbs.

Ingredients listed as optional are not included in the nutrition analysis.

When ingredient choices appear, we use the first one for the analysis.

Test Kitchen tips and sugar substitutes information are listed after the how-to steps.

Precise serving sizes help you manage portions.

tomato-ranch bean dip

12 g carb

SERVINGS 10 (2 tablespoons dip and ½ cup vegetable dippers each)
START TO FINISH 20 minutes

¼ cup dried tomatoes (not oil-pack)
1 15-ounce can cannellini beans (white kidney beans), rinsed and drained
½ cup bottled reduced-calorie ranch salad dressing
2 cloves garlic, minced
½ teaspoon finely chopped chipotle chile pepper in adobo sauce (optional)*
¼ cup snipped fresh parsley
5 cups carrot sticks, sweet pepper strips, celery sticks, zucchini sticks, broccoli florets, and/or cauliflower florets

1. Place tomatoes in a small bowl. Add enough boiling water to cover. Let stand for 5 minutes. Drain and finely chop the tomatoes; set aside.
2. In a food processor, combine beans, salad dressing, garlic, and chipotle pepper (if using). Cover and process until smooth. Set aside 1 teaspoon of the tomatoes and 1 teaspoon of the parsley for garnish. Stir remaining tomatoes and parsley into bean mixture.
3. Transfer to a serving bowl. Top with reserved tomatoes and parsley. Serve with assorted vegetable dippers.

*TEST KITCHEN TIP: Because chile peppers contain volatile oils that can burn your skin and eyes, avoid direct contact with them as much as possible. When working with chile peppers, wear plastic or rubber gloves. If your bare hands do touch the peppers, wash your hands and nails well with soap and warm water.

PER SERVING: 81 cal., 3 g total fat (0 g sat. fat), 3 mg chol., 242 mg sodium, 12 g carb., 4 g fiber, 3 g pro. Exchanges: 0.5 vegetable, 0.5 starch, 0.5 fat. Carb choices: 1.

Key to abbreviations used in the nutrition information:

cal. = calories
carb. = carbohydrate
chol. = cholesterol
pro. = protein
sat. fat = saturated fat

For marinades, we assume most of it is discarded.

When we list a range in the number of servings, we base the analysis on the smaller number.

Ingredients
- Tub-style vegetable oil spread refers to 60% to 70% vegetable oil product.
- Lean ground beef refers to 95% or leaner ground beef.

Serving sizes

These symbols, used with our recipes, indicate the size of a single serving.

Cup

For foods you ladle or spoon, such as soup or pasta.

Round pan

For foods served in wedges, such as cake, pizza, and quiche.

Rectangular dish

For foods cooked in casserole dishes and baking pans, such as lasagna, sheet cake, and bars.

breakfast favorites

Start your day off right with a delicious yet easy-to-make breakfast. Whether you need something quick on a busy morning or a special dish for a weekend brunch, you'll find the perfect recipe here.

Make It Lighter

Eat breakfast. The morning meal may help you eat less later in the day and can kick-start your metabolism so your body burns calories at a higher rate.

bacon 'n' egg pockets

18 g
carb

SERVINGS 4 (1 pita half each) **START TO FINISH** 15 minutes

- 2 eggs
- 4 egg whites
- 3 ounces Canadian-style bacon, chopped
- 3 tablespoons water
- 2 tablespoons sliced green onion (optional)
- ⅛ teaspoon salt
- Nonstick cooking spray
- 2 large whole wheat pita bread rounds, halved crosswise
- ½ cup shredded reduced-fat cheddar cheese (2 ounces; optional)

1. In a medium bowl, combine eggs, egg whites, Canadian bacon, water, green onion (if desired), and salt. Beat with a wire whisk or rotary beater until well mixed.
2. Lightly coat an unheated large nonstick skillet with nonstick cooking spray. Preheat over medium heat. Add egg mixture to skillet. Cook, without stirring, until mixture begins to set on the bottom and around edge. Using a spatula or a large spoon, lift and fold the partially cooked egg mixture so the uncooked portion flows underneath. Continue cooking for about 2 minutes or until egg mixture is cooked through but is still glossy and moist. Remove from heat immediately.
3. Fill pita halves with egg mixture. If desired, sprinkle with cheese.

NUTRITION FACTS PER SERVING: 162 cal., 4 g total fat (1 g sat. fat), 118 mg chol., 616 mg sodium, 18 g carb., 2 g fiber, 13 g pro. Exchanges: 1 starch, 1.5 very lean meat, .5 fat. Carb choices: 1.

quick and easy omelet

7 g carb

SERVINGS 4 (¼ omelet each)   **START TO FINISH** 20 minutes

Nonstick cooking spray
2 cups refrigerated or frozen egg product, thawed, or 8 eggs
2 tablespoons snipped fresh chives, Italian (flat-leaf) parsley, or chervil
⅛ teaspoon salt
⅛ teaspoon cayenne pepper
½ cup shredded reduced-fat sharp cheddar cheese (2 ounces)
2 cups fresh baby spinach leaves or torn fresh spinach
1 recipe Red Pepper Relish (see below)

1. Coat a 10-inch nonstick skillet with flared sides with nonstick cooking spray. Heat skillet over medium heat.
2. In a large bowl, combine the eggs, chives, salt, and cayenne pepper. Use rotary beater or wire whisk to beat until frothy. Pour into prepared skillet. Immediately begin stirring the egg mixture gently but continuously with a wooden or plastic spatula until mixture resembles small pieces of cooked egg surrounded by liquid egg. Stop stirring. Cook for 30 to 60 seconds more or until eggs are set but shiny.
3. Sprinkle with cheese. Top with 1 cup of the spinach and ¼ cup of the Red Pepper Relish. With a spatula, lift and fold one side of omelet partially over filling. Arrange remaining spinach on warm platter. Transfer omelet to platter. Top with remaining relish.

red pepper relish: In a small bowl, combine ⅔ cup chopped red sweet pepper, 2 tablespoons finely chopped green onion or onion, 1 tablespoon cider vinegar, and ¼ teaspoon black pepper.

NUTRITION FACTS PER SERVING: 122 cal., 3 g total fat (2 g sat. fat), 10 mg chol., 404 mg sodium, 7 g carb., 3 g fiber, 16 g pro. Exchanges: 2 very lean meat, 1.5 vegetable, .5 fat. Carb choices: .5.

mushroom scrambled eggs

5 g carb

SERVINGS 4 (⅔ cup each)   **START TO FINISH** 25 minutes

Nonstick cooking spray
- ½ cup sliced fresh mushrooms
- ¼ cup thinly sliced green onions
- 1 teaspoon cooking oil
- 1 18-ounce carton refrigerated or frozen egg product, thawed, or 4 eggs, beaten
- ¼ cup fat-free milk
- ⅛ teaspoon black pepper
- ½ cup shredded reduced-fat cheddar cheese (2 ounces) or ¼ cup crumbled reduced-fat feta or blue cheese (1 ounce)
- 1 slice turkey bacon, crisp-cooked and crumbled
- 8 grape or cherry tomatoes, halved

1. Coat an unheated large nonstick skillet with nonstick cooking spay. Preheat skillet over medium heat. Add mushrooms and green onions. Cook and stir for 5 to 7 minutes or until vegetables are tender. Stir in oil.
2. In a medium bowl, stir together eggs, milk, and pepper. Pour egg mixture into skillet. Cook, without stirring, until mixture begins to set on the bottom and around edge. Using a large spoon or spatula, lift and fold partially cooked egg mixture so uncooked portion flows underneath.
3. Sprinkle with cheese and bacon. Continue cooking over medium heat for 2 to 3 minutes or until egg mixture is cooked through but is still glossy and moist. Remove from heat immediately. (Be careful not to overcook the egg mixture.)
4. To serve, top with tomatoes.

NUTRITION FACTS PER SERVING: 102 cal., 5 g total fat (2 g sat. fat), 13 mg chol., 286 mg sodium, 5 g carb., 1 g fiber, 11 g pro. Exchanges: 1.5 very lean meat, .5 vegetable, 1 fat. Carb choices: .5.

southwestern breakfast tostadas

26 g
carb

SERVINGS 2 (½ tostada stack each)   **START TO FINISH** 20 minutes

- 2 6-inch corn tortillas
- ½ cup canned black beans, rinsed and drained
- 2 eggs
- 1 tablespoon fat-free milk
- ⅛ teaspoon black pepper
- ⅛ teaspoon salt
  Nonstick cooking spray
- ½ medium tomato, sliced
- 2 tablespoons shredded queso fresco or reduced-fat Monterey Jack cheese
- 2 teaspoons snipped fresh cilantro
  Light sour cream (optional)
  Chopped fresh cilantro (optional)

1. Warm tortillas according to package directions. Meanwhile, in a small bowl, use a potato masher or fork to slightly mash beans; set aside. In another small bowl or 1-cup glass measure, combine eggs, milk, pepper, and salt; beat with a rotary beater or wire whisk.

2. Lightly coat an unheated medium nonstick skillet with nonstick cooking spray. Preheat over medium heat. Pour egg mixture into hot skillet. Cook, without stirring, until egg mixture begins to set on the bottom and around edge. With a spatula or large spoon, lift and fold the partially cooked egg mixture so the uncooked portion flows underneath. Cook for 2 to 3 minutes more or until egg mixture is cooked through but is still glossy and moist. Immediately remove from heat.

3. Spread one tortilla with mashed beans. Top with the remaining tortilla, cooked egg mixture, tomatoes, cheese, and snipped cilantro. If desired, top with a dollop of sour cream and chopped cilantro. Serve immediately.

NUTRITION FACTS PER SERVING: 213 cal., 7 g total fat (2 g sat. fat), 217 mg chol., 446 mg sodium, 26 g carb., 5 g fiber, 12 g pro. Exchanges: 2 starch, 1 lean meat, .5 fat. Carb choices: 2.

shrimp-artichoke frittata

6 g carb

SERVINGS 4 (1 wedge each)   **START TO FINISH** 30 minutes

4 ounces fresh or frozen shrimp in shells
½ of a 9-ounce package frozen artichoke hearts
2 cups refrigerated or frozen egg product, thawed
¼ cup fat-free milk
¼ cup thinly sliced green onions
⅛ teaspoon garlic powder
⅛ teaspoon black pepper
Nonstick cooking spray
3 tablespoons finely shredded Parmesan cheese
Cherry tomatoes, quartered (optional)
Italian (flat-leaf) parsley (optional)

1. Thaw shrimp, if frozen. Peel and devein shrimp. Rinse shrimp; pat dry. Halve shrimp lengthwise; set aside. Meanwhile, cook artichoke hearts according to package directions; drain. Cut artichoke hearts into quarters; set aside.
2. Stir together egg product, milk, green onions, garlic powder, and pepper; set aside.
3. Lightly coat a large nonstick skillet with nonstick cooking spray. Heat skillet until a drop of water sizzles. Add shrimp to skillet; cook shrimp for 1 to 3 minutes or until shrimp turn opaque.
4. Pour egg mixture into skillet; do not stir. Place skillet over medium-low heat. As the egg mixture sets, run a spatula around the edge of the skillet, lifting edges to allow liquid to run underneath. Continue cooking and lifting edges until mixture is almost set (top will be wet).
5. Remove skillet from heat; sprinkle artichoke pieces evenly over the top. Sprinkle with Parmesan cheese. Let stand, covered, for 3 to 4 minutes or until top is set. Loosen edges of frittata. Transfer to a serving plate; cut into 4 wedges to serve. If desired, garnish with cherry tomatoes and parsley.

NUTRITION FACTS PER SERVING: 126 cal., 3 g total fat (1 g sat. fat), 37 mg chol., 343 mg sodium, 6 g carb., 2 g fiber, 19 g pro. Exchanges: 2 lean meat, .5 vegetable. Carb choices: .5.

omelet Provençal

10 g carb

SERVINGS 2 (1 omelet each) **START TO FINISH** 30 minutes

  Nonstick cooking spray
2 cups sliced fresh mushrooms
3 tablespoons sliced green onions
1 clove garlic, minced
1 cup refrigerated or frozen egg product, thawed, or 4 eggs, lightly beaten
¼ teaspoon herbes de Provence or dried thyme or basil, crushed
⅛ teaspoon salt
  Pinch of black pepper
1 teaspoon olive oil
¼ cup shredded part-skim mozzarella cheese (1 ounce)
1 medium plum tomato, chopped
1 tablespoon finely shredded Asiago or Parmesan cheese
  Fresh basil or parsley leaves (optional)

1. Lightly coat an unheated 6- to 7-inch nonstick skillet with flared sides with nonstick cooking spray. Preheat skillet over medium heat. Add mushrooms, green onions, and garlic; cook and stir until mushrooms are tender. Using a slotted spoon, remove mushroom mixture from skillet; set aside. If necessary, drain skillet; carefully wipe out skillet with paper towels.
2. In a medium bowl, combine eggs, herbes de Provence, salt, and pepper.
3. Add half of the oil to the skillet; heat skillet over medium heat. Pour half of the egg mixture into skillet. Using a wooden or plastic spatula, immediately begin stirring the eggs gently but continuously until mixture resembles small pieces of cooked egg surrounded by liquid egg. Stop stirring. Cook for 30 to 60 seconds more or until egg mixture is set and shiny.
4. Sprinkle with half of the mozzarella cheese. Top with half of the mushroom mixture. Continue cooking until cheese just begins to melt. Using the spatula, lift and fold an edge of the omelet partially over filling. Remove from skillet; cover and keep warm.
5. Repeat with remaining oil, egg mixture, mozzarella cheese, and mushroom mixture. Top omelets with tomato, Asiago cheese, and (if desired) fresh basil.

NUTRITION FACTS PER SERVING: 168 cal., 6 g total fat (3 g sat. fat), 13 mg chol., 512 mg sodium, 10 g carb., 2 g fiber, 20 g pro. Exchanges: 2.5 lean meat, 1.5 vegetable, .5 fat. Carb choices: 1.

Make It Count

Measure your breakfast grains, such as grits, oatmeal, and cereal. Overestimating by just ⅓ cup can add 100 calories.

cheesy grits and sausage

SERVINGS 4 (about 1 cup each)   **START TO FINISH** 25 minutes

30 g carb

- 4 cups water
- 1 cup quick-cooking grits
- 4 ounces bulk turkey sausage, cooked and drained
- 2 tablespoons sliced green onion
- 4 teaspoons finely chopped, seeded fresh jalapeño chile pepper*
- ½ teaspoon garlic salt
- ⅛ teaspoon black pepper
- ¼ cup shredded reduced-fat cheddar cheese (1 ounce)

1. In a medium saucepan, bring water to boiling. Slowly add grits, stirring constantly. Return to boiling; reduce heat. Cook and stir for 5 to 7 minutes or until the water is absorbed and mixture is thickened.
2. Stir in turkey sausage, green onion, chile pepper, garlic salt, and black pepper. Sprinkle individual servings with cheese.

*TEST KITCHEN TIP: Because chile peppers contain volatile oils that can burn your skin and eyes, avoid direct contact with them as much as possible. When working with chile peppers, wear plastic or rubber gloves. If your bare hands do touch the peppers, wash your hands and nails well with soap and warm water.

NUTRITION FACTS PER SERVING: 226 cal., 7 g total fat (2 g sat. fat), 42 mg chol., 444 mg sodium, 30 g carb., 2 g fiber, 12 g pro. Exchanges: 2 starch, 1 medium-fat meat. Carb choices: 2.

vegetarian cream cheese and bagels

31 g carb

SERVINGS 4 (1 bagel half each) **START TO FINISH** 30 minutes

½ of an 8-ounce tub light cream cheese (½ cup)
1 tablespoon snipped fresh dill or 1 teaspoon dried dill
¼ teaspoon salt
⅛ teaspoon black pepper
4 whole wheat bagel halves, toasted, or 4 slices whole wheat bread, toasted
½ of a medium cucumber, thinly sliced
½ of a medium onion, thinly sliced
½ of a medium avocado, halved, pitted, peeled, and thinly sliced
¾ cup bottled roasted red sweet peppers, drained and cut into thin strips
Fresh dill sprigs (optional)

In a small bowl, stir together cream cheese, snipped or dried dill, salt, and black pepper. Spread bagel halves with cream cheese mixture. Top with cucumber slices, onion slices, avocado slices, and red pepper strips. If desired, top with dill sprigs.

NUTRITION FACTS PER SERVING: 222 cal., 8 g total fat (3 g sat. fat), 13 mg chol., 301 mg sodium, 31 g carb., 5 g fiber, 9 g pro. Exchanges: 1.5 starch, 1 vegetable, 1.5 fat. Carb choices: 2.

Make It Count

Top sandwiches with a slice
of avocado instead of cheese
and you'll get a dose of healthy
monounsataurated fatty acids
instead of the saturated fat found
in the cheese. You'll also get folate
and fiber, which can help reduce
your risk of heart disease.

blueberry buckwheat pancakes

11 g
carb

SERVINGS 12 (1 pancake each)   **START TO FINISH** 30 minutes

½ cup buckwheat flour
½ cup whole wheat flour
1 tablespoon sugar*
½ teaspoon baking powder
¼ teaspoon baking soda
¼ teaspoon salt
1¼ cups buttermilk or sour milk**

¼ cup refrigerated or frozen egg product, thawed, or 1 egg, slightly beaten
1 tablespoon cooking oil
¼ teaspoon vanilla
¾ cup fresh or frozen blueberries

1. In a medium bowl, stir together buckwheat flour, whole wheat flour, sugar, baking powder, baking soda, and salt. Make a well in center of flour mixture; set aside. In a small bowl, combine buttermilk, egg product, oil, and vanilla. Add buttermilk mixture all at once to flour mixture. Stir until just combined but still slightly lumpy. Stir in blueberries.
2. Heat a lightly greased griddle or heavy skillet over medium heat until a few drops of water sprinkled on griddle dance across the surface. For each pancake, pour a scant ¼ cup batter onto hot griddle. Spread batter into a circle about 4 inches in diameter.
3. Cook over medium heat until pancakes are browned, turning to cook second sides when pancake surfaces are bubbly and edges are slightly dry (1 to 2 minutes per side). Serve immediately or keep warm in a loosely covered ovenproof dish in a 300°F oven.

*SUGAR SUBSTITUTES: Choose from Splenda granulated or Sweet'N Low bulk or packets. Follow package directions to use product amount equivalent to 1 tablespoon sugar.

**TEST KITCHEN TIP: To make 1¼ cups sour milk, place 4 teaspoons lemon juice or vinegar in a 2-cup glass measuring cup. Add enough fat-free milk to make 1¼ cups total liquid; stir. Let the mixture stand for 5 minutes before using.

NUTRITION FACTS PER SERVING: 66 cal., 2 g total fat (0 g sat. fat), 1 mg chol., 122 mg sodium, 11 g carb., 1 g fiber, 3 g pro. Exchanges: .5 starch. Carb choice: 1.
PER SERVING WITH SUGAR SUBSTITUTE: same as above, except 62 cal., 10 g carb., 2 g sugar. Carb choices: .5.

stuffed French toast

22 g carb

SERVINGS 8 (1 piece French toast each)   **START TO FINISH** 25 minutes

½ cup light tub-style cream cheese (about 5 ounces)
2 tablespoons low-sugar strawberry or apricot preserves
8 1-inch slices French bread
2 egg whites
1 egg, slightly beaten
¾ cup fat-free milk
½ teaspoon vanilla
⅛ teaspoon apple pie spice
Nonstick cooking spray
½ cup low-sugar strawberry or apricot preserves

1. In a small bowl, combine cream cheese and 2 tablespoons preserves. Using serrated knife, form pocket in each bread slice by making a horizontal cut halfway between top and bottom crust, slicing not quite all the way through. Fill each pocket with about 1 tablespoon of the cream cheese mixture.
2. In a small bowl, combine egg whites, egg, milk, vanilla, and apple pie spice. Lightly coat nonstick griddle with nonstick cooking spray; heat over medium heat.
3. Dip stuffed bread slices into egg mixture, coating both sides. Place bread slices on hot griddle. Cook for about 3 minutes or until golden brown, turning once.
4. Meanwhile, in small saucepan, heat ½ cup preserves until melted, stirring frequently. Serve over French toast.

TEST KITCHEN TIP: To make ahead, stuff each bread slice and place in an airtight container. Cover; refrigerate overnight. In the morning, prepare egg mixture and cook.

NUTRITION FACTS PER SERVING: 144 cal., 3 g total fat (2 g sat. fat), 34 mg chol., 245 mg sodium, 22 g carb., 1 g fiber, 6 g pro. Exchanges: 1 starch, .5 other carb, 1 fat. Carb choices: 1.

Make It Count

Add a few walnuts to your cereal. Walnuts have more omega-3 fatty acids than any other type of nut. Some studies have found that omega-3 fatty acids may help increase insulin sensitivity in people with type 2 diabetes.

walnut waffles
with blueberry sauce

33 g carb

SERVINGS 8 (½ of a square waffle or ¾ of a round waffle and about 3 tablespoons sauce each)

PREP 15 minutes   **BAKE** per waffle baker directions

- 1   cup all-purpose flour
- 1   cup whole wheat flour
- ¼   cup coarsely ground toasted walnuts
- 2   teaspoons baking powder
- 1   teaspoon baking soda
- 4   egg whites
- 2¼ cups buttermilk
- 2   tablespoons cooking oil
- 1   recipe Blueberry Sauce (see below)

1. In a medium bowl, stir together all-purpose flour, whole wheat flour, walnuts, baking powder, and baking soda. In a large bowl, beat egg whites with an electric mixer on medium speed until very foamy. Stir in buttermilk and oil. Gradually add flour mixture, beating by hand until smooth.
2. Pour 1 cup of the batter (for square waffle baker) or ⅔ cup of the batter (for round waffle baker) onto grids of a preheated, lightly greased waffle baker. Close lid quickly; do not open lid until waffle is done. Bake according to manufacturer's directions. When done, use a fork to lift waffle off grids. Repeat with remaining batter. Serve waffles warm with Blueberry Sauce.

blueberry sauce: In a medium saucepan, combine 1 cup fresh or frozen blueberries, ¼ cup white grape juice, and 1 tablespoon honey. Heat just until bubbles form around edges. Cool slightly. Transfer to a blender. Cover and blend until smooth. Transfer sauce to a serving bowl. Stir in 1 cup fresh or frozen blueberries. Makes about 1⅔ cups.

NUTRITION FACTS PER SERVING: 224 cal., 7 g total fat (1 g sat. fat), 3 mg chol., 359 mg sodium, 33 g carb., 4 g fiber, 8 g pro. Exchanges: 1 starch, 1 other carb, 1 fat. Carb choices: 2.

spiced Irish oatmeal

SERVINGS 6 (½ cup each)   **PREP** 5 minutes   **START TO FINISH** 15 minutes

- 3 cups water
- 1 cup steel-cut oats
- 1 tablespoon packed brown sugar*
- ¼ teaspoon ground cinnamon
- ⅛ teaspoon salt
- ⅛ teaspoon ground allspice
- Pinch of ground cloves or ground nutmeg
- 3 cups fat-free milk

1. In a 2-quart saucepan, combine water, oats, brown sugar, cinnamon, salt, allspice, and cloves or nutmeg.

2. Bring to boiling; reduce heat. Simmer, uncovered, for 10 to 15 minutes or until desired doneness and consistency, stirring occasionally. Serve with milk.

*****SUGAR SUBSTITUTES:** Choose from Sweet'N Low brown or Sugar Twin granulated brown. Use 1½ teaspoons Sweet'N Low brown or 1 tablespoon Sugar Twin granulated brown to substitute for the brown sugar.

NUTRITION FACTS PER SERVING: 158 cal., 2 g total fat (0 g sat. fat), 2 mg chol., 106 mg sodium, 27 g carb., 3 g fiber, 9 g pro. Exchanges: 1.5 starch, .5 milk. Carb choices: 2
PER SERVING WITH BROWN SUGAR SUBSTITUTE: 149 cal., 2 g total fat (0 g sat. fat), 2 mg chol., 106 mg sodium, 24 g carb., 3 g fiber, 9 g pro. Exchanges: .5 milk, 1.5 starch. Carb choices: 1.5

Make It Count

Before you eat your next bowl of breakfast cereal, grab dry and wet measuring cups. If you keep track of diabetes exchanges as part of your meal plan, one serving of cereal is ½ cup and one serving of milk is 1 cup.

Q&A
grains, fruits, & more

The experts at *Diabetic Living* magazine answer common questions about health, nutrition, and meal planning.

You often hear that eating oats can help prevent heart disease, but what about diabetes?

A: Studies show that eating any type of whole grain, including oats, can improve insulin sensitivity for people with insulin resistance or type 2 diabetes. That means the body's own insulin will respond more efficiently to high blood glucose.

Whole grains contain soluble fiber, such as oats and barley, can smooth out how quickly glucose from food enters your blood stream so the blood glucose level doesn't rise too fast or too high after you eat. Other food sources of soluble fiber include beans, whole wheat and bran cereals, apples, oranges, carrots, and other fruits and vegetables. Whole grains also have insoluble fiber to keep your digestive system healthy, as well as many different antioxidants. That's why the USDA 2005 Dietary Guidelines recommends at least three daily servings of whole grain foods. Simply replace the refined grains you eat for your carbohydrate servings with whole grains. Trade in white bread for whole wheat, or white rice for barley.

Q: Why do you give so many recipes that have fruits? I can't eat fruit because it raises my blood glucose.

A: Before you give up on fruit, carefully examine your meals and the portions you eat. People with diabetes often worry about eating fruit because it has sugar. But as with any source of carbohydrate, the sugar is converted to glucose in the body for energy. As long as the fruit you eat fits with the amount of carbohydrate in your meal plan, you should be able to enjoy fruit or foods that include fruit. The Dietary Guidelines recommend 2 cups of fruit per day for most average-size adults. Fruit provides a good source of energy, vitamins, minerals, and fiber (except for juice, which does not provide fiber). If fresh fruit is expensive in your area, you can choose fruit that is canned or dried with no sugar.

If your blood glucose is rising too high after you eat fruit, check your portion sizes. One serving of fruit has 15 grams of carbohydrate and 60 calories. Serving sizes are: a small piece of whole fruit, half of a large piece of fruit, and about ½ cup of canned or packaged fruit.

> The truth is that we all need to eat foods with carbohydrate because they supply the energy our bodies need to function.

Q: I've been told to choose protein-rich foods over foods high in carbohydrate in order to help manage my weight and blood glucose levels. Why is that?

A: For good health, our bodies require a balance of all the main nutrients: carbohydrate, protein, and fat. But when weight loss or blood glucose control is at stake, carbohydrate-containing foods tend to be perceived as the enemy. The truth is that we all need to eat foods with carbohydrate because they supply the energy our bodies need to function. But carbohydrate is quickly digested and can cause a spike in blood glucose levels. Protein takes longer to digest so it doesn't cause as big a rise in blood glucose after eating.

Replacing some of the carbohydrate in your diet with protein can help lower your blood glucose levels, especially if you're replacing simple carbs such as white bread or sugary drinks. Keep in mind that when you increase the protein in your meals, you tend to increase the fat as well, because protein-rich foods usually contain some fat. Higher fat intake can lead to weight gain, high cholesterol, and increased insulin resistance. Another important thing to keep in mind is total caloric intake. Regardless of the percentage of protein, fat, and carbohydrate in your diet, if your total calories are excessive for your needs, weight gain will occur.

quick-fix sandwiches

Instead of the same old grilled cheese
or tuna salad, build your sandwich a new way.
With unique flavors, interesting fillings,
and a variety of breads, these recipes will put
an end to your boring sandwich days.

chicken, spinach, and pear pitas

24 g carb

SERVINGS 6 (1 pita half each)   **START TO FINISH** 30 minutes

12 ounces skinless, boneless chicken breast halves
1 tablespoon balsamic vinegar
3 whole wheat pita bread rounds, halved crosswise
¼ cup light mayonnaise
1 ounce soft goat cheese (chèvre)

1 tablespoon fat-free milk
1 teaspoon balsamic vinegar
1 green onion, thinly sliced
1½ cups fresh spinach leaves
1 small pear or apple, cored and thinly sliced

1. Brush chicken on both sides with some of the 1 tablespoon balsamic vinegar; set aside. Grill chicken on the rack of an uncovered grill directly over medium coals. Grill 12 to 15 minutes or until chicken is no longer pink (170°F), turning once and brushing with the remainder of the 1 tablespoon vinegar halfway through grilling. (For a gas grill, preheat grill. Reduce heat to medium. Place chicken on the grill rack over heat. Cover and grill as above.) Cut each chicken breast half into ½-inch-thick slices.

2. Meanwhile, wrap pita bread rounds in foil. Place on the grill rack directly over medium coals. Grill about 8 minutes or until bread is warm, turning once halfway through grilling.

3. For sauce: In a small bowl, use a fork to stir together mayonnaise, goat cheese, milk, and the 1 teaspoon balsamic vinegar. Stir in green onion.

4. To assemble, arrange spinach, pear slices, and chicken in pita bread halves. Spoon about 1 tablespoon sauce into each pita.

NUTRITION FACTS PER SERVING: 216 cal., 6 g total fat (2 g sat. fat), 39 mg chol., 293 mg sodium, 24 g carb., 3 g fiber, 18 g pro. Exchanges: 1.5 starch, 2 lean meat. Carb choices: 1.5.

Make It Count

Use fresh spinach leaves on sandwiches instead of lettuce or saute it in a little olive oil and garlic for a quick side dish. Spinach contains lutein and zeaxanthin, two immune-boosting antioxidants important for eye health.

Make It Fast

Grill extra chicken breasts and use them for the next day for a different recipe. Chop them up for a salad, use to make a quick soup, or fold into a high-fiber tortilla for a fast wrap.

grilled chicken sandwiches

SERVINGS 4 (1 sandwich each)   **START TO FINISH** 30 minutes

26 g carb

- ¼ cup light mayonnaise
- ½ teaspoon finely shredded lime or lemon peel
- 1 medium zucchini or yellow summer squash, cut lengthwise into ¼-inch-thick slices*
- 3 tablespoons Worcestershire sauce for chicken
- 4 skinless, boneless chicken breast halves (1 to 1¼ pounds total)
- 4 whole wheat hamburger buns, split and toasted

1. For lime dressing: In a small bowl, combine mayonnaise and lime peel. Cover and chill until serving time.
2. Brush zucchini slices with 1 tablespoon of the Worcestershire sauce; set aside. Brush all sides of chicken with the remaining 2 tablespoons Worcestershire sauce.
3. Place chicken on the rack of an uncovered grill directly over medium coals. Grill 12 to 15 minutes or until no longer pink (170°F), turning once halfway through grilling. Add zucchini slices to grill for the last 6 minutes of grilling time for chicken, turning once and grilling until zucchini slices are softened and lightly browned.
4. To serve, spread lime dressing onto cut sides of toasted buns. If desired, halve zucchini slices crosswise. Place zucchini and chicken slices on bun bottoms; add bun tops.

*TEST KITCHEN TIP: For added color, use half of a medium zucchini and half of a medium yellow summer squash.

NUTRITION FACTS PER SERVING: 297 cal., 7 g total fat (1 g sat. fat), 71 mg chol., 469 mg sodium, 26 g carb., 3 g fiber, 31 g pro. Exchanges: 1.5 starch, 3.5 lean meat, .5 vegetable. Carb choices: 2.

chicken, kraut, and apple panini

20 g carb

SERVINGS 4 (1 sandwich each)   **START TO FINISH** 30 minutes

- 1 cup canned sauerkraut
- 8 very thin slices firm-texture whole wheat bread
  Nonstick cooking spray
- 12 ounces sliced cooked chicken breast
- 1 apple, cored and thinly sliced
- 4 thin slices Swiss cheese (2 to 3 ounces total)

1. Place sauerkraut in a colander and rinse with cold water. Drain well, using a spoon to press out excess liquid. Set aside.

2. Lightly coat one side of each bread slice with nonstick cooking spray. Place 4 bread slices, coated sides down, on a work surface. Top with sauerkraut, chicken, apple slices, and cheese. Top with remaining 4 bread slices, coated sides up.

3. Coat an unheated grill pan or large skillet with nonstick cooking spray. Preheat over medium-low heat for 1 to 2 minutes. Add sandwiches, in batches if necessary. Place a heavy skillet atop sandwiches. Cook over medium-low heat for 6 to 8 minutes or until bottoms are toasted. Using hot pads, carefully remove top skillet. Turn sandwiches and top again with skillet. Cook for 6 to 8 minutes more or until bottoms are toasted.

NUTRITION FACTS PER SANDWICH: 290 cal., 8 g total fat (4 g sat. fat), 85 mg chol., 464 mg sodium, 20 g carb., 4 g fiber, 33 g pro. Exchanges: 1 starch, 4 lean meat, 1 fat. Carb choices: 1.

dried tomato–pepper spread: In a small bowl, combine ¼ cup dried tomatoes (not oil-pack) and 2 tablespoons boiling water. Cover and let stand for 5 minutes. Transfer undrained tomato mixture to a food processor. Add ¼ cup drained bottled roasted red sweet peppers; 1 tablespoon balsamic vinegar; ½ teaspoon snipped fresh oregano or ¼ teaspoon dried oregano, crushed; 1 clove garlic, minced; and a pinch of ground black pepper. Cover and process until smooth. Makes ⅓ cup.

Mediterranean chicken panini

35 g carb

SERVINGS 4 (1 panini each)   **START TO FINISH** 30 minutes

Nonstick cooking spray
2 small skinless, boneless chicken breast halves (about 8 ounces total)
1 recipe Dried Tomato–Pepper Spread (see left)
4 miniature squares whole wheat bagel bread or multigrain ciabatta rolls, split
1 small zucchini

1. Lightly coat an unheated panini griddle, covered indoor electric grill, or large nonstick skillet with nonstick cooking spray. Preheat over medium heat or heat according to manufacturer's directions. Add chicken. If using griddle or grill, close lid and grill for 6 to 7 minutes or until chicken is no longer pink. (If using skillet, cook chicken for 10 to 12 minutes or until chicken is no longer pink, turning once.) Cool chicken slightly; split each chicken piece in half horizontally and cut crosswise into 2-inch-wide slices.

2. Spread the Dried Tomato–Pepper Spread on cut sides of bread. Place chicken on bottoms of the bread squares. Using a vegetable peeler, cut very thin lengthwise strips from the zucchini. Place zucchini strips on top of the chicken. Place bagel square tops on top of the zucchini, spread sides down. Press down lightly. Lightly coat the top and bottom of each sandwich with nonstick cooking spray.

3. Place sandwiches on griddle, grill, or skillet, adding in batches if necessary. If using griddle or grill, close lid and grill for 2 to 3 minutes or until bread is toasted. (If using skillet, place a heavy saucepan or skillet on top of sandwiches. Cook for 1 to 2 minutes or until bottoms are toasted. Carefully remove saucepan or top skillet; it may be hot. Turn sandwiches; top again with the saucepan or skillet. Cook for 1 to 2 minutes more or until bread is toasted.)

NUTRITION FACTS PER SERVING: 238 cal., 2 g total fat (0 g sat. fat), 354 mg sodium, 35 g carb., 5 g fiber, 21 g pro. Exchanges: 2 starch, 1.5 lean meat, 1 vegetable. Carb choices: 2.

Greek-style turkey burgers

22 g carb

SERVINGS 4 (1 burger, 1 pita half, and about ⅓ cup Olive-Tomato Salsa each)
START TO FINISH 30 minutes

⅓ cup fine dry whole wheat bread crumbs*
1 egg white, lightly beaten
1 tablespoon plain low-fat yogurt
1 teaspoon snipped fresh rosemary or ½ teaspoon dried rosemary, crushed
1 teaspoon snipped fresh oregano or ½ teaspoon dried oregano, crushed

⅓ cup crumbled reduced-fat feta cheese
⅛ teaspoon black pepper
1 pound uncooked ground turkey breast or chicken breast
   Mixed torn salad greens (optional)
1 recipe Olive-Tomato Salsa
   Plain low-fat yogurt (optional)
2 whole wheat pita bread rounds, halved and lightly toasted

1. In a medium bowl, combine bread crumbs, egg white, yogurt, rosemary, oregano, 1 tablespoon of the feta cheese, and the pepper. Add turkey; mix well. Shape turkey mixture into four ¾-inch-thick patties.
2. Place patties on the greased rack of an uncovered grill directly over medium coals. Grill for 12 to 14 minutes or until no longer pink (165°F), turning once halfway through grilling.
3. If desired, divide greens among 4 serving plates; top with burgers. Top burgers with Olive-Tomato Salsa, the remaining feta cheese, and (if desired) additional yogurt. Serve burgers with pita bread.

*TEST KITCHEN TIP: For fine dry whole wheat bread crumbs: Place 1 slice whole wheat bread, toasted, in a food processor. Cover and process until fine crumbs form. Measure ⅓ cup.

olive-tomato salsa: In a small bowl, stir together 1 cup chopped, seeded tomatoes; ¼ cup chopped, seeded cucumber; ¼ cup chopped, pitted kalamata or other ripe olives; ½ teaspoon snipped fresh rosemary or ¼ teaspoon dried rosemary, crushed; and ½ teaspoon snipped fresh oregano or ¼ teaspoon dried oregano, crushed. Makes about 1½ cups.

NUTRITION FACTS PER SERVING: 265 cal., 5 g total fat (1 g sat. fat), 59 mg chol., 523 mg sodium, 22 g carb., 4 g fiber, 33 g pro. Exchanges: 1.5 starch, 4 lean meat. Carb choices: 1.5.

Cajun turkey sandwich

19 g carb

SERVINGS 4 (1 sandwich each) **START TO FINISH** 20 minutes

⅓ cup light mayonnaise or salad dressing
1 teaspoon purchased salt-free Cajun seasoning or Homemade Salt-Free Cajun Seasoning (see below)
1 clove garlic, minced
8 very thin slices firm-texture whole wheat bread, toasted if desired
1 cup fresh spinach leaves
8 ounces packaged lower-sodium sliced turkey breast
4 tomato slices
1 small green sweet pepper or fresh poblano chile pepper,* seeded and sliced

1. In a small bowl, stir together mayonnaise, Cajun seasoning, and garlic. Spread on one side of each of the bread slices.
2. To assemble, place 4 of the bread slices, spread sides up, on serving plates. Layer with spinach, turkey, tomato slices, and sweet pepper or chile pepper. Top with remaining bread slices, spread sides down. Cut in half to serve.

*See tip on page 27.

homemade salt-free cajun seasoning: In a small bowl, stir together ¼ teaspoon white pepper, ¼ teaspoon garlic powder, ¼ teaspoon onion powder, ¼ teaspoon paprika, ¼ teaspoon black pepper, and ⅛ to ¼ teaspoon cayenne pepper.

NUTRITION FACTS PER SERVING: 210 cal., 9 g total fat (1 g sat. fat), 37 mg chol., 635 mg sodium, 19 g carb., 3 g fiber, 16 g pro. Exchanges: 1 starch, 1.5 lean meat, .5 vegetable. Carb choices: 1.

Make It Fast

Warm tortillas quickly and easily by wrapping them tightly in foil and then placing them in a 300°F oven for about 5 minutes. The foil keeps them from drying out.

beef and black bean wraps

30 g carb

SERVINGS 6 (1 wrap each)　**START TO FINISH** 25 minutes

- 8　ounces lean ground beef
- 1　cup chopped onion
- 2　cloves garlic, minced
- 1½　teaspoons ground cumin
- 1　teaspoon chili powder
- ½　teaspoon ground coriander
- 1　15-ounce can black beans, rinsed and drained
- 1　large tomato, chopped
- ¼　teaspoon black pepper
- 6　8-inch whole wheat flour tortillas
- 1½　cups shredded lettuce
- 1　to 1½ cups shredded reduced-fat cheddar or
  Monterey Jack cheese (4 to 6 ounces)
  Salsa (optional)

1. In a large skillet, cook ground beef, onion, and garlic for 5 minutes or until meat is brown. Drain off fat.
2. Stir in cumin, chili powder, and coriander. Cook and stir for 1 minute. Stir in black beans, tomato, and pepper. Cook, covered, for 5 minutes more, stirring occasionally.
3. To serve, spoon beef mixture down the center of each tortilla. Sprinkle with lettuce and cheese. Roll up. If desired, serve with salsa.

NUTRITION FACTS PER SERVING: 310 cal., 11 g total fat (5 g sat. fat), 35 mg chol., 651 mg sodium, 30 g carb., 15 g fiber, 24 g pro. Exchanges: 2 starch, 2.5 lean meat, .5 vegetable, .5 fat. Carb choices: 2.

open-face barbecue tilapia sandwiches

13 g carb

SERVINGS 4 (1 piece fish, 1 slice bread, and about ½ cup cabbage mixture and 1½ teaspoons barbecue sauce each) **START TO FINISH** 20 minutes

4 4- to 5-ounce fresh or frozen skinless tilapia or flounder fillets
   Nonstick cooking spray
2 tablespoons light mayonnaise
2 teaspoons lemon juice
2 cups packaged shredded cabbage with carrot (coleslaw mix)
4 slices whole wheat bread, toasted
2 tablespoons bottled low-calorie barbecue sauce

1. Thaw fish, if frozen. Rinse fish; pat dry with paper towels. Measure thickness of fish. Lightly coat both sides of each fish fillet with nonstick cooking spray.
2. Place fish on the greased rack of an uncovered grill directly over medium coals. Grill for 4 to 6 minutes per ½-inch thickness or until fish flakes easily when tested with a fork. (For a gas grill, preheat grill. Reduce heat to medium. Place fish on greased grill rack over heat. Cover and grill as above.)
3. In a medium bowl, stir together mayonnaise and lemon juice. Add cabbage; toss to coat.
4. To assemble, spoon cabbage mixture onto bread slices. Top with fish fillets. Drizzle fish with barbecue sauce.

NUTRITION FACTS PER SERVING: 206 cal., 5 g total fat (1 g sat. fat), 59 mg chol., 339 mg sodium, 13 g carb., 2 g fiber, 26 g pro. Exchanges: 1 starch, 3 lean meat, .5 vegetable. Carb choices: 1.

Make It Count

Go beyond the usual tomato and lettuce and top a sandwich with high-fiber slaw, nutrient-packed spinach, and/or flavorful roasted red sweet pepper strips.

grilled Jamaican jerk fish wraps

23 g carb

SERVINGS 4 (1 wrap each)　**START TO FINISH** 30 minutes

- 1 pound fresh or frozen skinless flounder, cod, or sole fillets
- 1½ teaspoons Jamaican jerk seasoning
- 4 7- to 8-inch whole grain flour tortillas
- 2 cups packaged fresh baby spinach
- ¾ cup chopped seeded tomato
- ¾ cup chopped fresh mango or pineapple
- 2 tablespoons snipped fresh cilantro
- 1 tablespoon finely chopped seeded fresh jalapeño chile pepper*
- 1 tablespoon lime juice

1. Thaw fish, if frozen. Rinse fish; pat dry with paper towels. Sprinkle Jamaican jerk seasoning over both sides of each fish fillet; rub in with your fingers. Measure thickness of fish.
2. Grill tortillas on the greased rack of an uncovered grill directly over medium coals for 1 minute or until bottoms of tortillas have grill marks. Remove from grill and set aside. Place fish on the grill rack directly over the coals. Grill fish for 4 to 6 minutes per ½-inch thickness or until fish flakes easily when tested with a fork, turning once halfway through grilling. (For a gas grill, preheat grill. Reduce heat to medium. Place tortillas on greased grill rack over heat. Cover; grill as above. Remove tortillas from the grill and add fish; cover and grill as above.) Coarsely flake the fish.
3. Meanwhile, in a medium bowl, toss together spinach, tomato, mango, cilantro, chile pepper, and lime juice.
4. To assemble, place tortillas, grill mark sides down, on a flat work surface. Divide spinach mixture and fish among tortillas. Roll up tortillas to enclose filling. Cut each in half to serve.

*See tip on page 27.

NUTRITION FACTS PER SERVING: 254 cal., 4 g total fat (1 g sat. fat), 48 mg chol., 509 mg sodium, 23 g carb., 11 g fiber, 29 g pro. Exchanges: 1 starch, 3.5 lean meat, 1 vegetable. Carb choices: 1.5.

open-face egg sandwiches

SERVINGS 4 (1 open-face sandwich each)   START TO FINISH 15 minutes

17 g carb

- 1 cup frozen shelled sweet soybeans (edamame), thawed
- 1 small avocado, halved, pitted, and peeled
- 2 tablespoons lemon juice
- 2 cloves garlic, minced
- ¼ teaspoon salt
- ½ cup chopped red sweet pepper
- 4 very thin slices firm-texture whole wheat bread, toasted, or 2 whole wheat pita bread rounds, split in half horizontally
- 4 hard-cooked eggs, thinly sliced*
  Black pepper

1. In a medium bowl, combine edamame, avocado, lemon juice, garlic, and salt; use a fork or potato masher to mash ingredients together until avocado is smooth and edamame is coarsely mashed. Stir in sweet pepper.

2. Spread about ⅓ cup edamame mixture atop bread slices or on pita halves. Arrange egg slices atop edamame mixture. Sprinkle with black pepper.

*TEST KITCHEN TIP: To save time, look for hard-cooked eggs in the deli section or salad bar area of your supermarket.

NUTRITION FACTS PER SERVING: 240 cal., 14 g total fat (3 g sat. fat), 212 mg chol., 293 mg sodium, 17 g carb., 6 g fiber, 14 g pro. Exchanges: 1 starch, 2.5 medium-fat meat. Carb choices: 1.

Make It Count

Serve tuna, egg, or chicken salad wrapped in lettuce or raw cabbage leaves instead of bread to save carbs. Or stuff the salad into a hollowed out tomato or raw bell pepper, or serve on top of thick cucumber slices.

cheesy eggplant burgers

19 g carb

SERVINGS 6 (1 eggplant burger, 1 slice bread, and 1 slice cheese each)
START TO FINISH 20 minutes

- 1 teaspoon garlic powder
- ½ teaspoon black pepper
- ⅛ teaspoon salt
- ½ cup chopped seeded tomatoes
- 2 tablespoons olive oil
- 1 tablespoon snipped fresh oregano
- 2 teaspoons snipped fresh thyme
- 2 teaspoons cider vinegar
- 6 ½-inch-thick slices eggplant
- 6 ¾-ounce slices smoked Gouda cheese
- 6 ½-inch-thick slices whole grain baguette-style bread, toasted

1. In a small bowl, combine garlic powder, pepper, and salt. In another small bowl, combine half of the garlic powder mixture, the tomatoes, 1 tablespoon of the oil, the oregano, thyme, and vinegar. Set aside.
2. Brush eggplant slices with remaining 1 tablespoon oil and sprinkle with remaining garlic powder mixture.
3. Grill eggplant slices on the rack of an uncovered grill directly over medium coals for 6 to 8 minutes or just until tender and golden brown, turning once halfway through grilling and topping with the cheese slices for the last 2 minutes of grilling. (For a gas grill, preheat grill. Reduce heat to medium. Place eggplant slices on grill rack over heat. Cover and grill as above, topping with cheese as directed.)
4. Place eggplant slices on top of toasted bread slices. Top with tomato mixture.

NUTRITION FACTS PER SERVING: 201 cal., 11 g total fat (4 g sat. fat), 17 mg chol., 506 mg sodium, 19 g carb., 4 g fiber, 7 g pro. Exchanges: 1 starch, .5 high-fat meat, 1 vegetable, 1 fat. Carb choices: 1.

soy bacon and pesto wraps

24 g
carb

SERVINGS 4 (1 wrap each)   **START TO FINISH** 30 minutes

½ of a 10- to 12-ounce package fresh or frozen shelled sweet soybeans
   (edamame), thawed (about 1 cup)
1 medium fresh jalapeño chile pepper, seeded and chopped*
2 tablespoons snipped fresh cilantro
2 tablespoons lemon juice
2 tablespoons water
1 clove garlic, halved
4 slices soy bacon or turkey bacon
4 8-inch whole wheat flour tortillas or vegetable-flavored flour tortillas
2 cups torn mixed salad greens
2 medium tomatoes, seeded and chopped

1. If using fresh, cook edamame according to package directions. Drain; rinse
with cold water. Drain again. In a food processor, combine edamame, chile
pepper, cilantro, lemon juice, water, and garlic. Cover and process until
smooth. Set aside.

2. Cook bacon according to package directions. Drain well on paper towels.
Chop bacon.

3. To assemble, spread about ¼ cup of the edamame mixture on each tortilla.
Top with salad greens, tomatoes, and bacon, placing these ingredients on
edge of each tortilla. Roll up to enclose filling. Secure with a toothpick or
wrap ends in plastic wrap or foil to hold together. Cut in half to serve.

*See tip on page 27.

NUTRITION FACTS PER SERVING: 222 cal., 7 g total fat (1 g sat. fat), 0 mg chol.,
502 mg sodium, 24 g carb., 13 g fiber, 16 g pro. Exchanges: 1 starch,
2 lean meat, 1 vegetable, .5 fat. Carb choices: 1.5.

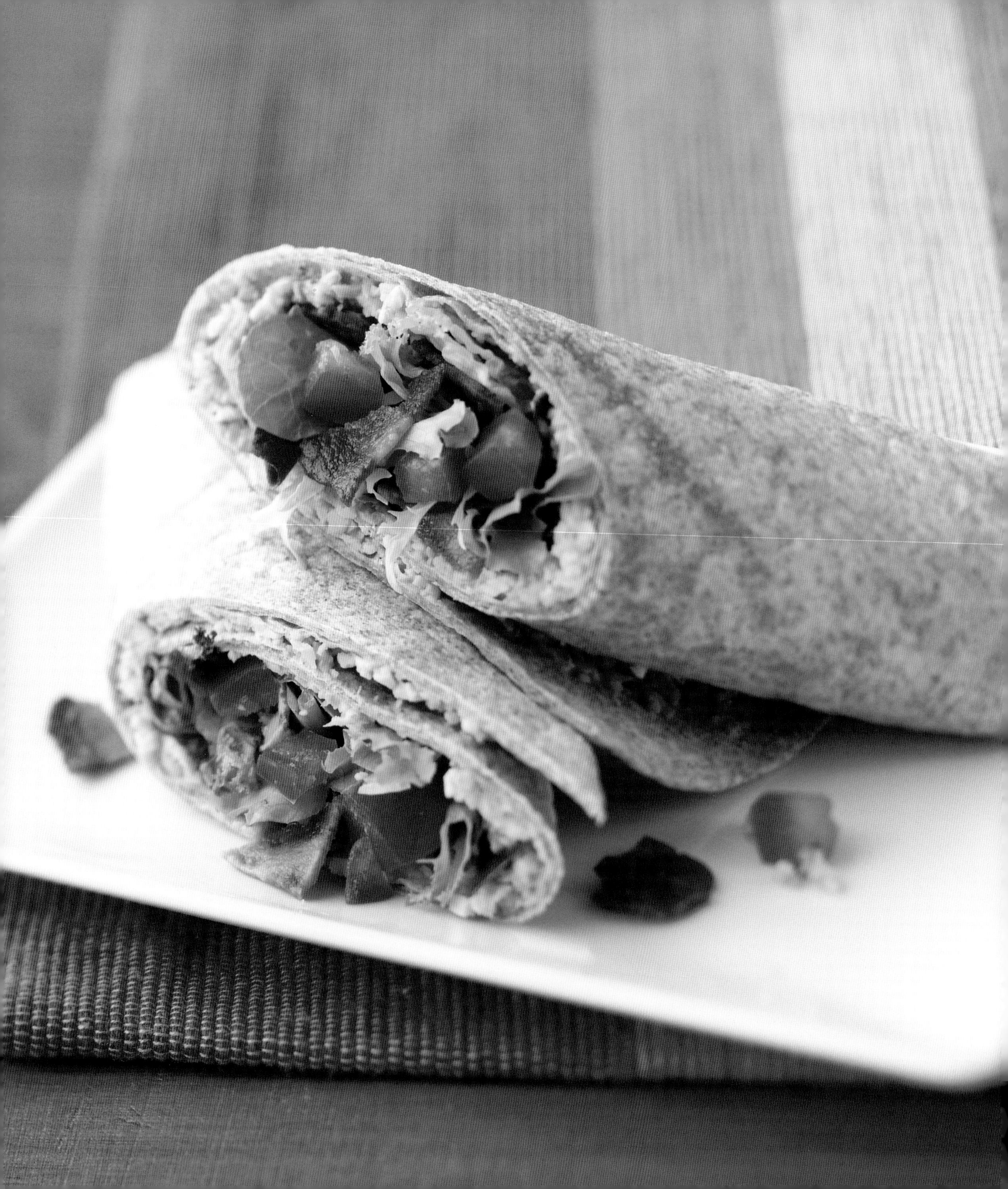

hearty
soups&stews

Why buy high-sodium canned soups when
it's so easy to make your own healthier
versions at home? Loaded with nutrient-rich
vegetables, fiber-rich beans, and nutty
whole grains, these soups and stews make
a filling and complete meal.

hamburger soup

16 g carb

SERVINGS 8 (1½ cups each)   **START TO FINISH** 30 minutes

- 8 ounces extra-lean ground beef
- 8 ounces ground turkey breast
- 2 medium onions, finely chopped
- 2 medium carrots, coarsely shredded
- 2 stalks celery, sliced
- 2 cloves garlic, minced
- 6 cups reduced-sodium beef broth
- 2 14½-ounce cans diced tomatoes, undrained
- 1 tablespoon snipped fresh sage or 1 teaspoon dried sage, crushed
- 2 teaspoons snipped fresh thyme or 1 teaspoon dried thyme, crushed
- 1 teaspoon snipped fresh rosemary or ½ teaspoon dried rosemary, crushed
- ¼ teaspoon salt
- ¼ teaspoon black pepper
- 2 medium potatoes, chopped (2 cups)
- Fresh sage (optional)

In a Dutch oven, combine beef, turkey, onion, carrot, celery, and garlic; cook over medium-high heat until meat is brown and onion is tender. Drain off fat. Stir broth, undrained tomatoes, fresh or dried sage, thyme, rosemary, salt, and pepper into beef mixture in Dutch oven. Bring to boiling; stir in potatoes. Reduce heat. Cover and simmer for 10 to 15 minutes or until vegetables are tender. If desired, garnish with additional fresh sage.

NUTRITION FACTS PER SERVING: 149 cal., 2 g total fat (1 g sat. fat), 31 mg chol., 631 mg sodium, 16 g carb., 2 g fiber, 16 g pro. Exchanges: 1 starch, 1.5 lean meat, 1 vegetable. Carb choices: 1.

chipotle chili with hominy and beans

35 g carb

SERVINGS 6 (1¼ cups each)   **START TO FINISH** 25 minutes

Nonstick cooking spray
- 8 ounces extra-lean ground beef, ground chicken breast, or ground turkey breast
- 1 cup chopped onion
- 1½ teaspoons ground cumin
- ½ teaspoon dried oregano, crushed
- 1 to 2 teaspoons chopped canned chipotle chile peppers in adobo sauce*
- 2 14½-ounce cans no-salt-added stewed tomatoes, undrained
- 1 15-ounce can red beans, rinsed and drained
- 1 15-ounce can yellow hominy, rinsed and drained
- 1 small green or red sweet pepper, seeded and chopped
- ½ cup water
- 6 tablespoons reduced-fat shredded cheddar cheese (optional)

1. Lightly coat an unheated large saucepan with nonstick cooking spray. Preheat over medium heat. Add ground beef and onion; cook until browned. If necessary, drain off fat.

2. Stir in cumin and oregano; cook for 1 minute more. Add chipotle peppers, undrained tomatoes, red beans, hominy, sweet pepper, and water. Bring to boiling; reduce heat. Cover and simmer for 5 minutes. Top with cheddar cheese to serve, if desired.

*See tip on page 27.

NUTRITION FACTS PER SERVING: 257 cal., 7 g total fat (3 g sat. fat), 26 mg chol., 477 mg sodium, 35 g carb., 9 g fiber, 13 g pro. Exchanges: 1.5 starch, 1.5 very lean meat, 1.5 vegetable, 1 fat. Carb choices: 1.5.

teriyaki beef soup

18 g carb

SERVINGS 5 (1⅓ cups each) **START TO FINISH** 30 minutes

- 8 ounces boneless top sirloin steak
- 2 teaspoons olive oil
- 1 large shallot, cut into thin rings
- 2 14-ounce cans lower-sodium beef broth
- 1 cup water
- ½ cup apple juice or apple cider
- 2 medium carrots, cut into thin bite-size strips (1 cup)
- ⅓ cup instant brown rice or quick-cooking barley
- 2 tablespoons light teriyaki sauce
- 1 tablespoon grated fresh ginger
- 3 cloves garlic, minced
- ¼ teaspoon crushed red pepper
- 2 cups coarsely chopped broccoli

1. If desired, partially freeze steak for easier slicing. Trim fat from steak. Cut steak into thin bite-size strips. In a large saucepan, heat oil over medium-high heat. Cook and stir steak and shallot in hot oil for 2 to 3 minutes or until beef is brown. Remove beef mixture with a slotted spoon; set aside.
2. In the same saucepan, combine broth, water, apple juice, carrots, rice or barley, teriyaki sauce, ginger, garlic, and crushed red pepper. Bring to boiling; reduce heat. Simmer, covered, for 10 minutes.
3. Stir in broccoli and the beef mixture. Bring to boiling; reduce heat. Simmer, covered, for 3 to 5 minutes or until rice and vegetables are tender.

NUTRITION FACTS PER SERVING: 162 cal., 4 g total fat (1 g sat. fat), 28 mg chol., 481 mg sodium, 18 g carb., 2 g fiber, 13 g pro. Exchanges: 1 starch, 1 lean meat, 1 vegetable. Carb choices: 1.

Asian pork soup

5 g carb

SERVINGS 5 (about 1¼ cups each)   **START TO FINISH** 25 minutes

- 1 tablespoon canola oil
- 12 ounces lean boneless pork, cut into thin bite-size strips
- 2 cups sliced fresh shiitake mushrooms
- 2 cloves garlic, minced
- 2 14-ounce cans reduced-sodium chicken broth
- 1¾ cups water
- 2 tablespoons dry sherry
- 2 tablespoons reduced-sodium soy sauce
- 2 teaspoons grated fresh ginger or ½ teaspoon ground ginger
- ¼ teaspoon crushed red pepper
- 2 cups shredded napa cabbage
- 1 green onion, thinly sliced

1. In a large saucepan, heat oil over medium heat. Add pork; cook and stir for 2 to 3 minutes or until slightly pink in center. Remove from pan; set aside. Add mushrooms and garlic to saucepan; cook until tender.

2. Stir in broth, water, sherry, soy sauce, ginger, and crushed red pepper. Bring to boiling. Stir in pork, cabbage, and green onion; heat through. If desired, garnish individual servings with cilantro.

NUTRITION FACTS PER SERVING: 164 cal., 7 g total fat (2 g sat. fat), 37 mg chol., 643 mg sodium, 5 g carb., 1 g fiber, 19 g pro. Exchanges: 2.5 lean meat, 1 vegetable, .5 fat. Carb choices: 0.

Make It Lighter

Make soup the main dish if you're watching your weight. It's largely liquid—causing a feeling of fullness, so you're less likely to fill up on side dishes or desserts. Just go easy on high-calorie and high-fat cream-base soups; opt for a broth base.

chicken tortilla soup

15 g carb

SERVINGS 4 (about 1½ cups each)   **START TO FINISH** 20 minutes

- 2 cups loose-pack frozen yellow, green, and red sweet peppers and onions stir-fry vegetables
- 1 14½-ounce can Mexican-style stewed tomatoes, undrained
- 1 14-ounce can reduced-sodium chicken broth
- 1¾ cups water
- 2 cups chopped cooked chicken breast (10 ounces)
- 2 cups packaged baked tortilla chips
- Jalapeño chile pepper slices (optional)

1. In a large saucepan, combine frozen vegetables, undrained tomatoes, broth, and water. Bring to boiling; reduce heat. Cover and simmer for 3 to 5 minutes or until vegetables are tender. Stir in chicken; heat through.

2. Ladle soup into warm soup bowls. Serve individual servings with tortilla chips. If desired, top with avocado and jalapeño.

NUTRITION FACTS PER SERVING: 222 cal., 3 g total fat (1 g sat. fat), 60 mg chol., 561 mg sodium, 15 g carb., 3 g fiber, 25 g pro.
Exchanges: .5 starch, 3 lean meat, 1.5 vegetable. Carb choices: 1.

chicken-squash noodle soup

20 g carb

SERVINGS 6 (1½ cups each)   **START TO FINISH** 30 minutes

- 1 tablespoon canola oil
- 1 medium onion, chopped
- 1 stalk celery, chopped
- 1 medium carrot, chopped
- 2 cloves garlic, minced
- ½ teaspoon poultry seasoning
- 3 14-ounce cans reduced-sodium chicken broth
- 1½ cups medium dried noodles
- 1 medium zucchini or yellow summer squash, quartered lengthwise and cut into 1-inch-thick pieces
- 1¾ cups fat-free milk
- ¼ cup all-purpose flour
- 2 cups cubed cooked chicken breast
- ¼ cup snipped fresh parsley

1. In 4-quart Dutch oven, heat oil over medium heat. Cook onion, celery, carrot, garlic, and poultry seasoning for about 5 minutes or just until tender, stirring occasionally. Add broth; bring to boiling. Add noodles and zucchini. Return to boiling; reduce heat. Cover and simmer for 5 minutes.

2. In a medium bowl, whisk milk and flour together until combined; stir into vegetable mixture. Add chicken. Cook and stir until bubbly. Cook and stir for 1 minute more. Sprinkle with parsley just before serving.

NUTRITION FACTS PER SERVING: 210 cal., 5 g total fat (1 g sat. fat), 49 mg chol., 555 mg sodium, 20 g carb., 2 g fiber, 22 g pro. Exchanges: 1 starch, 2.5 lean meat, .5 vegetable. Carb choices: 1.

Make It Count

Be quick when cooking garlic. Garlic exposed to high heat for more than 10 minutes loses important nutrients, such as allicin, which works as a potent anti-inflammatory and has been shown to help lower cholesterol and blood-pressure levels.

five-spice chicken noodle soup

14 g carb

SERVINGS 4 (1¼ cups each)   **START TO FINISH** 20 minutes

2½ cups water
1¼ cups reduced-sodium chicken broth
  2 green onions, thinly bias-sliced (¼ cup)
  2 teaspoons reduced-sodium soy sauce
  2 cloves garlic, minced
  ¼ teaspoon five-spice powder
  ⅛ teaspoon ground ginger
  2 cups chopped bok choy
  1 medium red sweet pepper, cut into thin bite-size strips
  2 ounces somen noodles, broken into 2-inch lengths, or 2 ounces
     fine dried noodles
1½ cups chopped cooked chicken breast (about 8 ounces)

In a large saucepan, combine water, broth, green onions, soy sauce, garlic,
five-spice powder, and ginger. Bring to boiling. Stir in bok choy, sweet pepper
strips, and somen. Return to boiling; reduce heat. Boil gently for 3 to 5
minutes or until noodles are just tender. Stir in cooked chicken. Heat through.

NUTRITION FACTS PER SERVING: 181 cal., 4 g total fat (1 g sat. fat),
51 mg chol., 556 mg sodium, 14 g carb., 1 g fiber, 20 g pro. Exchanges:
.5 starch, 2 very lean meat, 1.5 vegetable. Carb choices: 1.

Mexican-style turkey soup

15 g carb

SERVINGS 6 (about 1⅓ cups each) **START TO FINISH** 30 minutes

Nonstick cooking spray
1 cup chopped onion
1 large red sweet pepper, chopped
1 teaspoon ground cumin
1 teaspoon chili powder
½ teaspoon paprika
5 cups reduced-sodium chicken broth
1½ cups peeled cubed winter squash
1 large tomato, chopped
¼ teaspoon salt
¼ teaspoon black pepper
2 cups chopped cooked turkey breast or chicken breast (about 10 ounces)
1 cup loose-pack frozen whole kernel corn
2 tablespoons snipped fresh cilantro

1. Coat an unheated Dutch oven with nonstick cooking spray. Preheat over medium heat. Add onion and sweet pepper to hot Dutch oven. Cook for about 5 minutes or until tender, stirring occasionally. Stir in cumin, chili powder, and paprika; cook and stir for 30 seconds.

2. Add broth, squash, tomato, salt, and black pepper. Bring to boiling; reduce heat. Cover and simmer for about 20 minutes or until squash is tender, stirring occasionally. Stir in turkey or chicken, corn, and cilantro; heat through.

NUTRITION FACTS PER SERVING: 153 cal., 3 g total fat (1 g sat. fat), 35 mg chol., 615 mg sodium, 15 g carb., 3 g fiber, 17 g pro. Exchanges: .5 starch, 2 very lean meat, 1 vegetable, .5 fat. Carb choices: 1.

Make It Lighter

Cut just 100 calories a day and you'll lose more than 10 pounds a year. Up your cuts to 250 and you'll be down 26 pounds.

German potato-sausage soup

16 g carb

SERVINGS 6 (about 1⅓ cups each)   **START TO FINISH** 30 minutes

- 12 ounces bulk turkey sausage
- 8 ounces presliced fresh mushrooms
- 1 medium onion, chopped
- 1 stalk celery, chopped
- 1 teaspoon caraway seeds, crushed
- ¼ teaspoon black pepper
- 1¾ cups lower-sodium beef stock
- ½ cup light beer or nonalcoholic beer
- 2 medium potatoes, cubed
- 1 cup small broccoli florets
- 2 cups shredded green cabbage
- 1½ cups fat-free milk

1. In a 4-quart Dutch oven, cook sausage, mushrooms, onion, and celery over medium heat until sausage is browned, stirring to break up sausage as it cooks. Drain off fat.
2. Add caraway seeds and pepper to sausage mixture in Dutch oven. Add stock and beer; bring to boiling. Add potatoes. Cover and simmer for 10 minutes. Add broccoli. Cover and simmer for 5 minutes more or until potatoes and broccoli are tender.
3. Stir cabbage and milk into sausage-broccoli mixture. Cook for 2 to 3 minutes or just until cabbage is tender and soup is heated through.

NUTRITION FACTS PER SERVING: 179 cal., 5 g total fat (1 g sat. fat), 44 mg chol., 522 mg sodium, 16 g carb., 3 g fiber, 17 g pro. Exchanges: 1 starch, 2 lean meat, 1 vegetable. Carb choices: 1.

Asian shrimp and vegetable soup

9 g carb

SERVINGS 6 (about 1⅓ cups each)   **START TO FINISH** 30 minutes

- 4 green onions
- 2 teaspoons canola oil
- 2 medium carrots, thinly sliced
- 8 ounces fresh shiitake or oyster mushrooms, coarsely chopped
- 1 tablespoon grated fresh ginger or 1 teaspoon ground ginger
- 2 cloves garlic, minced
- 2 14-ounce cans reduced-sodium chicken broth
- 2 cups water
- 1 cup frozen shelled sweet soybeans (edamame)
- 1 tablespoon reduced-sodium soy sauce
- ¼ teaspoon crushed red pepper (optional)
- 8 ounces peeled, cooked large shrimp
- 1 cup fresh sugar snap peas, ends trimmed and strings removed, and/or coarsely shredded bok choy
  Slivered green onions (optional)

1. Diagonally slice whole green onions into 1-inch-long pieces, keeping white parts separate from green tops. Set green tops aside. In a large nonstick saucepan, heat oil over medium heat. Add white parts of green onions, the carrot, and mushrooms; cook for 5 minutes, stirring occasionally. Add ginger and garlic; cook and stir for 1 minute more.

2. Add broth, water, soybeans, soy sauce, and (if desired) crushed red pepper to mushroom mixture. Bring to boiling; reduce heat. Cover and simmer for 5 minutes or just until carrot is tender.

3. Add shrimp and pea pods and/or bok choy. Return to boiling; reduce heat. Simmer, uncovered, for 2 minutes or until heated through. Stir in green onion tops just before serving. If desired, garnish with slivered green onions.

NUTRITION FACTS PER SERVING: 128 cal., 4 g total fat (0 g sat. fat), 74 mg chol., 511 mg sodium, 9 g carb., 3 g fiber, 15 g pro. Exchanges: 2 lean meat, 1 vegetable. Carb choices: .5.

Italian fish stew

SERVINGS 4 (1½ cups each)   **START TO FINISH** 30 minutes

12 g carb

- 8 ounces fresh or frozen skinless cod or sea bass fillets
- 6 ounces fresh or frozen peeled and deveined shrimp
- 2 teaspoons olive oil
- ⅓ cup chopped onion
- 2 stalks celery, sliced
- ½ teaspoon bottled minced garlic (1 clove)
- 1 cup reduced-sodium chicken broth
- ¼ cup dry white wine or reduced-sodium chicken broth
- 1 14½-ounce can no-salt-added diced tomatoes, drained
- 1 8-ounce can no-salt-added tomato sauce
- 1 teaspoon dried oregano, crushed
- ¼ teaspoon salt
- ⅛ teaspoon black pepper
- 1 tablespoon snipped fresh Italian (flat-leaf) parsley

1. Thaw fish and shrimp, if frozen. Rinse fish and shrimp; pat dry with paper towels. Cut fish into 1½-inch pieces. Cut shrimp in half lengthwise. Cover and chill fish and shrimp until needed.

2. In a large saucepan, heat oil over medium heat. Cook onion, celery, and garlic in hot oil until tender. Carefully stir in broth and wine. Bring to boiling; reduce heat. Simmer, uncovered, for 5 minutes. Stir in tomatoes, tomato sauce, oregano, salt, and pepper. Return to boiling; reduce heat. Cover and simmer for 5 minutes.

3. Gently stir in fish and shrimp. Return just to boiling; reduce heat to low. Cover and simmer for 3 to 5 minutes or until fish flakes easily with a fork and shrimp are opaque. Sprinkle with parsley.

NUTRITION FACTS PER SERVING: 165 cal., 4 g total fat (1 g sat. fat), 87 mg chol., 459 mg sodium, 12 g carb., 2 g fiber, 19 g pro. Exchanges: 2 very lean meat, 2 vegetable, .5 fat. Carb choices: 1.

red bean stew

44 g carb

SERVINGS 4 (½ cup stew plus ½ cup rice each) **START TO FINISH** 20 minutes

- 1 teaspoon canola oil
- ⅔ cup chopped onion
- 3 cloves garlic, minced
- 1 cup water
- 2 tablespoons tomato paste
- 1 tablespoon snipped fresh cilantro
- 1 teaspoon snipped fresh oregano or ¼ teaspoon dried oregano, crushed
- ½ teaspoon adobo seasoning*
- 1 15-ounce can red kidney beans, rinsed and drained
- 2 cups hot cooked brown rice

  Fresh cilantro sprigs (optional)

1. In a large skillet, heat oil over medium heat. Add red onion and garlic; cook for 5 minutes or until onion is tender. Carefully add water, tomato paste, snipped cilantro, oregano, and adobo seasoning. Stir in beans. Bring to boiling; reduce heat. Cook and stir over medium heat for 5 to 10 minutes or until soup is slightly thickened, mashing beans slightly while stirring.

2. Serve stew with rice. If desired, garnish with cilantro sprigs.

*TEST KITCHEN TIP: Look for this seasoning blend at a market that specializes in Hispanic foods.

NUTRITION FACTS PER SERVING: 220 cal., 2 g total fat (0 g sat. fat), 0 mg chol., 427 mg sodium, 44 g carb., 8 g fiber, 11 g pro. Exchanges: 2.5 starch, .5 very lean meat. Carb choices: 3.

Make It Lighter
Start a meal with a salad or hot or cold vegetable soup to help you feel full and eat fewer total calories.

zesty gazpacho

SERVINGS 4 (2 cups each)   **PREP** 30 minutes   **CHILL** 2 to 24 hours

37 g carb

- 1 19-ounce can cannellini beans (white kidney beans), rinsed and drained
- 1 14½-ounce can Italian- or Mexican-style stewed tomatoes, undrained and cut up
- 2 cups tiny red pear-shaped or cherry tomatoes, halved or quartered
- 1 11½-ounce can low-sodium vegetable juice
- 1 cup water
- 1 cup coarsely chopped seeded cucumber
- ½ cup coarsely chopped yellow and/or red sweet pepper
- ¼ cup coarsely chopped red onion
- ¼ cup snipped fresh cilantro
- 3 tablespoons lime or lemon juice
- 2 cloves garlic, minced
- ¼ to ½ teaspoon bottled hot pepper sauce
   Lime wedges (optional)

In a large bowl, combine cannellini beans, undrained stewed tomatoes, fresh tomatoes, vegetable juice, water, cucumber, sweet pepper, red onion, cilantro, lime juice, garlic, and hot pepper sauce. Cover and chill for 2 to 24 hours. if desired, serve with lime wedges.

NUTRITION FACTS PER SERVING: 152 cal., 1 g total fat (0 g sat. fat), 0 mg chol., 605 mg sodium, 37 g carb., 10 g dietary fiber, 10 g pro. Exchanges: 1 starch, 3.5 vegetable. Carb choices: 2.5.

weeknight suppers

You'll find something for every taste in this versatile collection of simple suppers. And the best part? All of them can be ready to eat in 30 minutes or less—perfect for busy nights!

Make It Fast

Grill or roast meat, fish, or chicken to get your meal on the table quickly. These cooking methods use high heat so the food cooks rapidly. You also use less added fat than you would sautéing or frying the food.

apricot-glazed chicken kabobs

14 g
carb

SERVINGS 4 (1 skewer each)   **START TO FINISH** 30 minutes

 1 pound skinless, boneless chicken breast halves, cut into 1-inch pieces
1½ teaspoons Jamaican jerk seasoning
 1 cup fresh sugar snap peas or snow pea pods, ends trimmed and strings removed
 1 cup fresh or canned pineapple cubes
 1 medium red sweet pepper, seeded and cut into 1-inch pieces
 ¼ cup low-sugar apricot preserves

1. Sprinkle chicken with about half of the jerk seasoning; toss gently to coat. Cut any large pea pods in half crosswise.

2. Alternately thread chicken, sugar snap peas or pea pods, pineapple, and sweet pepper on 4 long (12-inch) skewers,* leaving a ¼-inch space between pieces.

3. In a small saucepan, combine remaining jerk seasoning and the preserves. Cook and stir just until preserves are melted; set aside.

4. Place kabobs on the rack of an uncovered grill directly over medium coals. Grill for 8 to 12 minutes or until chicken is no longer pink and vegetables are crisp-tender, turning once and brushing occasionally with sauce during the last 3 minutes of grilling.

*TEST KITCHEN TIP: If using wooden skewers, soak in enough water to cover for at least 1 hour before using.

NUTRITION FACTS PER SERVING: 184 cal., 2 g total fat (0 g sat. fat), 66 mg chol., 174 mg sodium, 14 g carb., 2 g fiber, 27 g pro. Exchanges: 1 other carbohydrates, 4 lean meat. Carb choices: 1.

pasta with chicken and broccoli

30 g carb

SERVINGS 6 (1⅔ cups each)   **START TO FINISH** 30 minutes

- 8 ounces whole grain or regular bowtie or penne pasta (about 2½ cups)
- 3 cups broccoli florets
- 4 skinless, boneless chicken breast halves (1 to 1¼ pounds total), cut into bite-size pieces
- 1 teaspoon adobo seasoning*
- 2 tablespoons olive oil
- 1 clove garlic, minced
- ¼ cup light mayonnaise or salad dressing
- ⅛ teaspoon black pepper
- 2 tablespoons finely shredded Parmesan cheese

1. In a Dutch oven, cook pasta according to package directions, except add broccoli for the last 5 minutes of cooking. Drain well. Return to hot pan.

2. Meanwhile, in a medium bowl, combine chicken pieces and adobo seasoning; toss to coat. In a large skillet, heat oil over medium-high heat; add garlic and cook for 30 seconds. Add chicken; cook for 3 to 4 minutes or until chicken is lightly brown and cooked through, stirring occasionally.

3. Add chicken to drained pasta and broccoli in Dutch oven. Stir in the mayonnaise and pepper. Cook over low heat until heated through, stirring occasionally.

4. To serve, top with shredded Parmesan cheese.

*****TEST KITCHEN TIP:** Look for this seasoning blend at a market that specializes in Hispanic foods.

NUTRITION FACTS PER SERVING: 309 cal., 9 g total fat (1 g sat. fat), 48 mg chol., 399 mg sodium, 30 g carb., 4 g fiber, 26 g pro. Exchanges: 2 starch, 2.5 very lean meat, .5 vegetable, 1 fat. Carb choices: 2.

lemon-thyme roasted chicken with fingerlings

21 g carb

SERVINGS 4 (1 chicken breast half and about ¾ cup potatoes each)

START TO FINISH 30 minutes

- 4 teaspoons canola or olive oil
- 1 teaspoon dried thyme, crushed
- ½ teaspoon kosher salt or ¼ teaspoon regular salt
- ¼ teaspoon black pepper
- 1 pound fingerling potatoes, halved lengthwise, or tiny new red or white potatoes, halved
- 4 small skinless, boneless chicken breast halves (1 to 1¼ pounds total)
- 2 cloves garlic, minced
- 1 lemon, thinly sliced

1. In a very large skillet, heat 2 teaspoons of the oil over medium heat. Stir ½ teaspoon of the thyme, the salt, and pepper into the oil. Add potatoes; toss to coat. Cover and cook for 12 minutes, stirring twice.

2. Stir potatoes; push to one side of the skillet. Add remaining 2 teaspoons oil. Arrange chicken breast halves on the other side of the skillet. Cook, uncovered, for 5 minutes.

3. Turn chicken. Spread garlic over chicken breast halves; sprinkle with remaining ½ teaspoon thyme. Arrange lemon slices on top of chicken. Cover and cook for 7 to 10 minutes more or until chicken is no longer pink (170°F) and potatoes are tender.

NUTRITION FACTS PER SERVING: 255 cal., 6 g total fat (1 g sat. fat), 66 mg chol., 307 mg sodium, 21 g carb., 3 g fiber, 29 g pro. Exchanges: 1.5 starch, 3.5 lean meat. Carb choices: 1.5.

mushroom and chicken stroganoff

29 g
carb

SERVINGS 6 (½ cup noodles and ⅔ cup chicken mixture each) **START TO FINISH** 25 minutes

- 1 8-ounce carton light sour cream
- 2 tablespoons all-purpose flour
- 1 tablespoon Worcestershire-style marinade for chicken
- ½ teaspoon dried thyme, crushed
- ½ teaspoon instant chicken bouillon granules
- ¼ teaspoon black pepper
- ½ cup water
- 1 tablespoon canola or olive oil
- 8 ounces fresh mushrooms, sliced
- 1 medium onion, chopped
- 2 cloves garlic, minced
- 2½ cups coarsely shredded cooked chicken
- 3 cups hot cooked wide noodles
- 1 tomato, chopped

1. In small bowl, combine ⅔ cup of the sour cream, the flour, Worcestershire-style marinade, thyme, bouillon granules, and pepper. Gradually stir in water until combined. Set aside.
2. In a very large skillet, heat the oil over medium-high heat. Cook the mushrooms, onion, and garlic until tender and any liquid has evaporated, stirring occasionally. Stir in chicken.
3. Add sour cream mixture to skillet; cook and stir until thickened and bubbly. Reduce heat; cook and stir for 2 minutes more.
4. Serve chicken mixture over noodles; top with dollops of the remaining sour cream and the chopped tomato.

NUTRITION FACTS PER SERVING: 322 cal., 12 g total fat (4 g sat. fat), 88 mg chol., 191 mg sodium, 29 g carb., 2 g fiber, 24 g pro. Exchanges: 1.5 starch, 2.5 lean meat, .5 vegetable, 1.5 fat. Carb choices: 2.

sage and cream turkey fettuccine

29 g carb

SERVINGS 2 (about ½ cup pasta and ¾ cup turkey mixture each)   **START TO FINISH** 30 minutes

- 2 ounces dried spinach and/or plain fettuccine
- ⅓ cup light sour cream
- 2 teaspoons all-purpose flour
- ¼ cup reduced-sodium chicken broth
- 1 teaspoon snipped fresh sage or ½ teaspoon dried sage, crushed
- ⅛ teaspoon black pepper
  Nonstick cooking spray
- 6 ounces turkey breast tenderloin, cut into bite-size strips
- ¼ teaspoon salt
- 1 cup sliced fresh mushrooms
- 2 green onions, sliced
- 1 clove garlic, minced
  Fresh sage sprigs (optional)

1. Cook pasta according to package directions; drain and set aside.

2. Meanwhile, in a small bowl, stir together sour cream and flour until smooth. Gradually stir in broth until smooth. Stir in snipped or dried sage and pepper; set aside.

3. Coat an unheated 8-inch skillet with nonstick cooking spray. Preheat over medium-high heat. Sprinkle turkey with salt. Add turkey, mushrooms, green onions, and garlic to hot skillet. Cook and stir for about 3 minutes or until turkey is no longer pink.

4. Stir sour cream mixture into turkey mixture in skillet. Cook and stir until thickened and bubbly. Cook and stir for 1 minute more. Serve turkey mixture over hot cooked pasta. If desired, garnish with sage sprigs.

NUTRITION FACTS PER SERVING: 275 cal., 5 g total fat (2 g sat. fat), 64 mg chol., 441 mg sodium, 29 g carb., 4 g fiber, 28 g pro. Exchanges: 1.5 starch, 3 lean meat, .5 vegetable. Carb choices: 2.

spiced bulgur with beef and mango

SERVINGS 4 (scant ½ cup bulgur and ⅔ cup toppings each)   **START TO FINISH** 30 minutes

- 1 cup reduced-sodium chicken broth
- ⅔ cup bulgur
- 1 clove garlic, minced
- ½ teaspoon ground cumin
- ¼ teaspoon ground coriander
- ⅛ teaspoon ground cinnamon
- ⅛ teaspoon cayenne pepper
- 6 ounces lower-sodium deli roast beef, cut into thin strips
- ½ of a medium mango, peeled, pitted, and coarsely chopped
- ½ cup fresh pea pods, ends trimmed, strings removed, and halved crosswise
- 2 green onions, sliced
- ¼ cup snipped fresh cilantro
- ¼ cup unsalted peanuts, chopped (optional)

1. In a 1½-quart microwave-safe casserole, combine broth, bulgur, garlic, cumin, coriander, cinnamon, and cayenne pepper. Microwave, covered, on high (100% power) for about 4 minutes or until mixture is boiling. Remove from microwave. Let stand for about 20 minutes or until bulgur is tender. Drain, if necessary.
2. Divide bulgur mixture among 4 serving bowls. Top with beef, mango, pea pods, green onions, cilantro, and (if desired) peanuts.

NUTRITION FACTS PER SERVING: 164 cal., 2 g total fat (1 g sat. fat), 26 mg chol., 421 mg sodium, 25 g carb., 5 g fiber, 13 g pro. Exchanges: 1.5 starch, 1.5 lean meat. Carb choices: 1.5.

beef and asparagus sauté

20 g carb

SERVINGS 4 (1 cup sauté mixture and about ⅓ cup rice each)   **START TO FINISH** 25 minutes

- 12 ounces fresh asparagus spears
- 1 pound lean beef sirloin or tenderloin, trimmed of fat and very thinly sliced*
- ½ teaspoon salt
- ⅛ teaspoon black pepper
  Nonstick cooking spray
- ½ cup coarsely shredded carrot
- 1 teaspoon dried herbes de Provence, crushed
- ½ cup dry Marsala
- ¼ teaspoon grated lemon peel
- 1½ cups hot cooked brown rice

1. Snap off and discard fibrous stem ends of asparagus. Bias-cut asparagus into 2-inch-long pieces; rinse and drain well. Set aside. Sprinkle beef with salt and pepper.
2. Coat an unheated large nonstick skillet with nonstick cooking spray. Preheat over medium-high heat. Cook and stir beef in hot skillet for 3 minutes. Add asparagus, carrot, and herbes de Provence; cook and stir for 2 minutes more. Add Marsala and lemon peel; reduce heat.
3. Cook, uncovered, for 3 to 5 minutes more or until beef is cooked through and asparagus is crisp-tender. Serve over hot cooked rice.

*TEST KITCHEN TIP: Partially freeze beef for easier slicing.

NUTRITION FACTS PER SERVING: 257 cal., 5 g total fat (2 g sat. fat), 54 mg chol., 368 mg sodium, 20 g carb., 3 g fiber, 27 g pro. Exchanges: 1 starch, 3 very lean meat, 1 vegetable, 1 fat. Carb choices: 1.

lemon-pepper steak

1 g carb

SERVINGS 4 (about 3 ounces each)   **START TO FINISH** 25 minutes

1   pound beef flank steak
4   teaspoons snipped fresh oregano
1½   teaspoons bottled minced garlic or 3 cloves, minced
1   teaspoon finely shredded lemon peel
1   teaspoon olive oil
¼   teaspoon black pepper
     Fresh oregano (optional)

1. Preheat broiler. Trim fat from steak. In a small bowl, stir together snipped oregano, garlic, lemon peel, oil, and pepper. Sprinkle mixture evenly over both sides of steak; rub in with your fingers.
2. Place on unheated rack of broiler pan. Broil 3 to 4 inches from heat for 15 to 18 minutes for medium (160°F), turning once halfway through broiling.
3. Thinly slice steak diagonally across grain. If desired, sprinkle with additional fresh oregano.

NUTRITION FACTS PER SERVING: 173 cal., 7 g total fat (2 g sat. fat), 37 mg chol., 63 mg sodium, 1 g carb., 0 g fiber, 25 g pro. Exchanges: 3.5 lean meat, .5 fat. Carb choices: 0.

Make It Fast

Partially freeze beef before cutting it into strips for stir-fry dishes. Freezing makes it easier to slice and helps you get thin, even strips that cook quickly.

sesame-orange beef

SERVINGS 4 (¾ cup beef mixture and ½ cup rice each)   **START TO FINISH** 25 minutes

41 g carb

- 8 ounces fresh green beans, trimmed and halved crosswise
- 2 teaspoons sesame seeds
- ½ cup orange juice
- 2 tablespoons reduced-sodium soy sauce
- 1 tablespoon toasted sesame oil
- 1 teaspoon cornstarch
- ½ teaspoon finely shredded orange peel

- Nonstick cooking spray
- ½ cup bias-sliced green onions
- 1 tablespoon grated fresh ginger
- 2 cloves garlic, minced
- 1 teaspoon cooking oil
- 12 ounces boneless beef sirloin steak, thinly sliced
- 2 cups hot cooked brown rice
- 2 oranges, peeled and sectioned or thinly sliced crosswise

1. In a covered medium saucepan, cook green beans in a small amount of boiling water for 6 to 8 minutes or until crisp-tender. Drain; set aside.

2. Meanwhile, in a small skillet, cook sesame seeds over medium heat for 1 to 2 minutes or until toasted, stirring frequently. Set aside.

3. In a small bowl, combine orange juice, soy sauce, sesame oil, cornstarch, and orange peel; set sauce aside.

4. Coat an unheated large nonstick skillet with nonstick cooking spray. Preheat over medium-high heat. Add green onions, ginger, and garlic to hot skillet; stir-fry for 1 minute. Add the precooked green beans; stir-fry for 2 minutes. Remove vegetables from skillet.

5. Carefully add oil to the hot skillet. Add beef; stir-fry for about 3 minutes or until desired doneness. Remove from skillet.

6. Stir sauce; add to skillet. Cook and stir until thickened and bubbly; cook and stir for 2 minutes more. Return meat and vegetables to skillet. Heat through, stirring to coat all ingredients with sauce. Serve over hot cooked brown rice. Top with orange sections and sprinkle with toasted sesame seeds.

NUTRITION FACTS PER SERVING: 348 cal., 10 g total fat (2 g sat. fat), 52 mg chol., 341 mg sodium, 41 g carb., 6 g fiber, 24 g pro. Exchanges: 1.5 starch, 2.5 lean meat, 1 vegetable, 1 fruit. Carb choices: 3.

pork with pear-maple sauce

29 g carb

SERVINGS 4 (about 3 ounces meat and ⅓ cup sauce each)   **START TO FINISH** 25 minutes

- 1 12- to 16-ounce pork tenderloin
- 2 teaspoons snipped fresh rosemary or ½ teaspoon dried rosemary, crushed
- 1 teaspoon snipped fresh thyme or ¼ teaspoon dried thyme, crushed
- ¼ teaspoon salt
- ¼ teaspoon black pepper
- 1 tablespoon olive or cooking oil
- 2 medium pears, peeled and coarsely chopped
- ¼ cup pure maple syrup or maple-flavored syrup
- 2 tablespoons dried tart red cherries, halved
- 2 tablespoons dry white wine or apple juice

1. Trim fat from meat. Cut meat into ¼-inch slices. In a medium bowl, combine rosemary, thyme, salt, and pepper. Add meat slices; toss to coat. In a large skillet, heat oil over medium heat. Cook meat, half at a time, for 2 to 3 minutes or until meat is slightly pink in center, turning once. Remove meat from skillet; set aside.
2. In the same skillet, combine pears, maple syrup, dried cherries, and wine or juice. Bring to boiling; reduce heat. Boil gently, uncovered, for about 3 minutes or just until pears are tender. Return meat to skillet with pears; heat through.
3. To serve, use a slotted spoon to transfer meat to a warm serving platter. Spoon the pear mixture over meat.

NUTRITION FACTS PER SERVING: 255 cal., 7 g total fat (2 g sat. fat), 60 mg chol., 179 mg sodium, 29 g carb., 3 g fiber, 19 g pro. Exchanges: 1 other carb., 2.5 lean meat, 1 fruit. Carb choices: 2.

Make It Lighter

Slow down when eating. Your brain needs 20 minutes from the time you eat to register that you're full. Waiting that little bit can help you pass up seconds or dessert. You'll feel just as satisfied, but you'll consume fewer calories.

pork chops primavera

26 g carb

SERVINGS 4 (1 pork chop and 1 cup bean mixture each)   **START TO FINISH** 20 minutes

- 2 slices turkey bacon, cut into 1-inch pieces
- 12 ounces fresh green beans, trimmed
- 5 tablespoons water
- 4 bone-in pork chops, ½ inch thick
- 1 tablespoon reduced-sodium soy sauce
- 2 teaspoons canola oil
- 3 tablespoons apple butter
- 1 cup red and/or yellow cherry and/or grape tomatoes

1. In a 12-inch nonstick skillet, cook bacon according to package directions. Remove from skillet; set aside.

2. Meanwhile, in a 2-quart microwave-safe dish, cook beans in 2 tablespoons water, covered, on high (100% power) for 4 minutes; stir once. Drain; set aside.

3. Brush chops with soy sauce. In the same skillet, heat oil over medium heat. Brown chops on both sides. Add apple butter and remaining water; reduce heat. Simmer, covered, for 5 minutes. Add beans, tomatoes, and bacon; cook, uncovered, for 3 to 5 minutes, until heated through.

NUTRITION FACTS PER SERVING: 307 cal., 7 g total fat (3 g sat. fat), 83 mg chol., 309 mg sodium, 26 g carb., 4 g fiber, 33 g pro. Exchanges: 1.5 other carb., 4 lean meat, 1 vegetable. Carb choices: 2.

chile-lime catfish with corn sauté

25 g carb

SERVINGS 4 (1 piece fish and ½ cup corn mixture each)   **PREP** 25 minutes
COOK 4 to 6 minutes per ½-inch thickness

- 4 4- to 5-ounce fresh or frozen skinless catfish, sole, or tilapia fillets
- 1 tablespoon lime juice
- 1 teaspoon ground ancho chile pepper or chili powder
- ¼ teaspoon salt
- 1 tablespoon canola oil
- 2⅔ cups loose-pack frozen gold and white whole kernel corn, thawed
- ¼ cup finely chopped red onion
- 2 teaspoons seeded and finely chopped fresh jalapeño chile pepper*
- 2 cloves garlic, minced
- 1 tablespoon snipped fresh cilantro
  Lime wedges (optional)

1. Thaw fish, if frozen. Rinse fish; pat dry with paper towels. In a small bowl, stir together lime juice, ancho chile pepper, and salt. Brush mixture evenly over both sides of each fish fillet. Measure thickness of fish.
2. In a large nonstick skillet, heat 2 teaspoons of the oil over medium-high heat. Add fish fillets to hot oil; cook for 4 to 6 minutes per ½-inch thickness or until fish flakes easily when tested with a fork, turning once halfway through cooking. Remove from skillet. Cover and keep warm.
3. In the same skillet, cook corn, onion, jalapeño, and garlic in the remaining 1 teaspoon oil for about 2 minutes or until vegetables are heated through and just starting to soften, stirring occasionally. Remove from heat. Stir in cilantro.
4. To serve, divide corn mixture among 4 serving plates. Top with fish. If desired, serve with lime wedges.

*See tip on page 27.

NUTRITION FACTS PER SERVING: 288 cal., 13 g total fat (2 g sat. fat), 53 mg chol., 216 mg sodium, 25 g carb., 3 g fiber, 21 g pro. Exchanges: 1.5 starch, 2.5 lean meat, 1 fat. Carb choices: 1.5.

Make It Fast

Cut cleanup time by cooking vegetables on the grill along with your protein. To prevent sticking, be sure to lightly coat the veggies with nonstick cooking spray before placing them on the grill or in a grill basket.

herbed fish
and vegetables

13 g carb

SERVINGS 2 (1 piece fish, about ⅔ cup vegetables, and 2 tablespoons mayonnaise mixture each)   **PREP** 20 minutes   **COOK** 6 minutes

- 2 6-ounce fresh or frozen skinless flounder, sole, cod, or perch fillets, ½ to ¾ inch thick
- 2 tablespoons assorted snipped fresh herbs (such as parsley, basil, oregano, and/or thyme)
- 1 cup matchstick-size pieces carrot
- 1 cup matchstick-size pieces zucchini and/or yellow summer squash
- ½ of a lemon, thinly sliced
- 3 tablespoons light mayonnaise
- 1 tablespoon thinly sliced green onion
- ¼ teaspoon finely shredded lemon peel
- 1 teaspoon lemon juice

1. Thaw fish, if frozen. Rinse fish; pat dry with paper towels. Using a sharp knife, make shallow bias cuts in the fish fillets, spacing cuts ¾ inch apart. Sprinkle herbs over fillets, tucking into cuts.
2. Place a steamer insert in a large deep saucepan or large skillet with a tight-fitting lid. Add water to the saucepan or skillet until just below the steamer insert. Bring water to boiling. Place carrot and squash in the steamer basket. Place fish on top of vegetables. Arrange lemon slices on top of fish. Cover and steam over medium heat for 6 to 8 minutes or until fish flakes easily when tested with a fork, adding more water as needed to maintain steam.
3. Meanwhile, in a small bowl, stir together mayonnaise, green onion, lemon peel, and lemon juice.
4. To serve, divide fish and vegetables among 2 serving plates. Serve with mayonnaise mixture.

NUTRITION FACTS PER SERVING: 270 cal., 10 g total fat (2 g sat. fat), 90 mg chol., 340 mg sodium, 13 g carb., 4 g fiber, 34 g pro. Exchanges: 4 lean meat, 1.5 vegetable, 1 fat. Carb choices: 1.

basil-lemon shrimp linguine

SERVINGS 4 (1½ cups each)   **START TO FINISH** 30 minutes

1 pound fresh or frozen large shrimp in shells
6 ounces dried linguine or fettuccine
½ teaspoon salt
8 ounces fresh asparagus spears, trimmed and cut diagonally into 1-inch pieces
   Nonstick cooking spray
2 cloves garlic, minced
1 cup assorted sweet pepper strips
¼ cup snipped fresh basil or 1 tablespoon dried basil, crushed
1 teaspoon finely shredded lemon peel
¼ teaspoon black pepper
¼ cup sliced green onions
2 tablespoons lemon juice
1 tablespoon olive oil
   Fresh basil sprigs (optional)
   Lemon wedges (optional)

1. Thaw shrimp, if frozen. Peel and devein shrimp, leaving tails intact if desired.
2. Cook pasta according to package directions in water with ¼ teaspoon of the salt, adding asparagus for the last 3 minutes of cooking; drain and return to pan. Cover and keep warm.
3. Meanwhile, lightly coat a large nonstick skillet with nonstick cooking spray. Heat over medium heat; add garlic; cook and stir for 15 seconds. Add pepper strips; cook and stir for 2 minutes or until crisp-tender. Add shrimp, dried basil (if using), lemon peel, remaining ¼ teaspoon salt, and black pepper. Cook and stir for 3 minutes or until shrimp turn opaque. Remove from heat.
4. Add shrimp mixture to pasta mixture. Add snipped fresh basil (if using), the green onions, lemon juice, and oil; toss gently to coat. Transfer to serving plates. If desired, garnish each serving with basil sprigs and/or lemon wedges.

NUTRITION FACTS PER SERVING: 336 cal., 6 g total fat (1 g sat. fat), 172 mg chol., 463 mg sodium, 39 g carb., 4 g fiber, 31 g pro. Exchanges: 2 starch, 3 very lean meat, 1 vegetable, 1 fat. Carb choices: 2.5.

Mexican-style shrimp pizza

22 g carb

SERVINGS 2 (1 pizza each)   **START TO FINISH** 30 minutes   **OVEN** 400°F

- 2 8-inch whole wheat or regular flour tortillas
- 1 teaspoon olive oil
- Nonstick cooking spray
- 1 cup thin, bite-size assorted sweet pepper strips
- ⅓ cup thinly sliced green onions
- ½ of a medium fresh jalapeño chile pepper, seeded and thinly sliced* (optional)
- 1 tablespoon water
- 2 to 3 tablespoons purchased green salsa
- 4 ounces peeled and deveined cooked medium shrimp
- ⅓ cup shredded reduced-fat Monterey Jack cheese
- 1 tablespoon snipped fresh cilantro

1. Preheat oven to 400°F. Brush both sides of each tortilla with oil; place on an ungreased baking sheet. Bake for about 10 minutes or until crisp, turning once.

2. Meanwhile, coat an unheated medium nonstick skillet with nonstick cooking spray. Preheat skillet over medium heat. Add sweet pepper, green onions, and (if desired) chile pepper. Cook for about 5 minutes or until nearly crisp-tender, stirring occasionally. Add water; cover and cook for 2 minutes more. Spread each tortilla with about 1 tablespoon of the green salsa. Top with cooked vegetable mixture and shrimp. Sprinkle with cheese. Bake for about 3 minutes or until cheese is melted and shrimp is heated through. Sprinkle with cilantro.

*See tip on page 27.

NUTRITION FACTS PER SERVING: 265 cal., 11 g total fat (5 g sat. fat), 127 mg chol., 407 mg sodium, 22 g carb., 3 g fiber, 20 g pro. Exchanges: 1.5 starch, 1.5 very lean meat, .5 high-fat meat, .5 vegetable, 1 fat. Carb choices: 1.5.

basil-buttered salmon

0 g carb

SERVINGS 4 (1 fillet and 1 teaspoon butter mixture each)   **START TO FINISH** 25 minutes

4	fresh or frozen skinless salmon, halibut, or sea bass fillets (about 1¼ pounds)
½	teaspoon salt-free lemon-pepper seasoning
2	tablespoons butter, softened
1	teaspoon snipped fresh lemon basil, regular basil, or dill or ¼ teaspoon dried basil or dill, crushed
1	teaspoon snipped fresh parsley or cilantro
¼	teaspoon finely shredded lemon or lime peel
	Roasted asparagus spears, optional
	Boiled red potatoes, optional
	Freshly grated parmesan cheese, optional

1. Thaw fish, if frozen. Rinse fish; pat dry with paper towels. Sprinkle with lemon-pepper seasoning.
2. Place fish on the greased unheated rack of a broiler pan. Turn any thin portions under to make uniform thickness. Broil 4 inches from the heat for 5 minutes. Carefully turn fish over. Broil for 3 to 7 minutes more or until fish flakes easily when tested with a fork.
3. Meanwhile, in a small bowl, stir together butter, basil, parsley, and citrus peel. To serve, spoon 1 teaspoon of the butter mixture on top of each fish piece. Cover and refrigerate remaining butter mixture for another use. If desired, serve salmon with asparagus, potatoes, and parmesan cheese.

NUTRITION FACTS PER SERVING: 294 cal., 19 g total fat (5 g sat. fat), 94 mg chol., 113 mg sodium, 0 g carb., 0 g fiber, 28 g pro. Exchanges: 4 lean meat, 1.5 fat. Carb choices: 0.

Make It Count

Choose wild salmon over farmed. Wild salmon tends to have fewer chemical contaminants (such as PCB) than farmed salmon. Salmon is a great source of omega-3 fatty acids, which have been linked to a reduced risk of heart disease, and cancer.

Make It Fast

Buy precut veggies when time is short. Produce aisles are filled with a variety of ready-to-use mixes of salad greens and precut vegetables that you can enjoy raw, steamed, or microwaved.

garden-style ravioli

38 g carb

SERVINGS 4 (1 cup each)   **START TO FINISH** 30 minutes

1   9-ounce package refrigerated light cheese ravioli
    Nonstick cooking spray
1   medium red sweet pepper, cut into long, thin strips
1   medium green sweet pepper, cut into long, thin strips
1   medium carrot, cut into long, thin strips
1   small onion, chopped
3   cloves garlic, minced
1   medium tomato, chopped
¼   cup reduced-sodium chicken or vegetable broth
1   tablespoon snipped fresh tarragon or 1 teaspoon dried tarragon,
    crushed, or 3 tablespoons snipped fresh basil or 2 teaspoons dried basil,
    crushed

1. Cook ravioli according to package directions, except omit any oil or salt.
   Drain. Return pasta to hot saucepan; cover and keep warm.
2. Meanwhile, coat an unheated large nonstick skillet with nonstick cooking
   spray. Preheat over medium-high heat. Add sweet peppers, carrot, onion,
   and garlic to hot skillet; cook and stir for about 5 minutes or until vegetables
   are tender. Stir in tomato, broth, and tarragon or basil. Cook and stir for about
   2 minutes more or until heated through.
3. Add vegetable mixture to the cooked ravioli; gently toss to combine.

NUTRITION FACTS PER SERVING: 248 cal., 6 g total fat (3 g sat. fat), 26 mg
chol., 380 mg sodium, 38 g carb., 2 g fiber, 13 g pro. Exchanges:
2 starch, 1 lean meat, 1 vegetable. Carb choices: 2.5.

udon noodles with tofu

39 g
carb

SERVINGS 6 (about 1¼ cups each)   **START TO FINISH** 25 minutes

- 8 ounces dried udon noodles or whole wheat linguine
- 2 6- to 8-ounce packages smoked teriyaki-flavored or plain firm tofu, cut into ½-inch pieces
- 1½ cups chopped cucumber
- 1 large carrot, cut into thin bite-size pieces
- ½ cup sliced green onions
- 1 recipe Ginger-Soy Vinaigrette (see below)

1. Cook pasta according to package directions; drain. Cool pasta slightly.
2. Meanwhile, in a large bowl, combine tofu, cucumber, carrot, and green onions. Add drained pasta; toss gently to mix.
3. Drizzle Ginger-Soy Vinaigrette onto cooked pasta mixture. Toss salad gently to coat.

ginger-soy vinaigrette: In a small bowl, whisk together 2 tablespoons rice vinegar or cider vinegar; 1 tablespoon toasted sesame oil; 2 teaspoons reduced-sodium soy sauce; 4 cloves minced garlic; 1 teaspoon grated fresh ginger; and ¼ teaspoon crushed red pepper. Makes ¼ cup.

NUTRITION FACTS PER SERVING: 231 cal., 4 g total fat (0 g sat. fat), 0 mg chol., 571 mg sodium, 39 g carb., 3 g fiber, 7 g pro. Exchanges: 2 starch, .5 medium-fat meat, .5 vegetable, .5 fat. Carb choices: 2.5.

Make It Count

Go meatless once or twice a week with a soy-base
dinner that uses tofu, tempeh, or edamame. Soy
is a great meat alternative. It packs a protein
punch with healthful fat and no cholesterol.

Q&A

carb and fat facts

The experts at *Diabetic Living* magazine answer common questions about health, nutrition, and meal planning.

Q What's the difference between starchy and non-starchy vegetables?

A: When you have diabetes, it's key to recognize that vegetables fall into two categories: non-starchy and starchy. Non-starchy vegetables contain few calories and carbohydrate: an average of 25 calories and 5 grams of carbohydrate per serving. They include leafy greens, peppers, broccoli, mushrooms, and green beans.

Starchy vegetables, such as winter squash, peas, and potatoes, are treated more like a traditional carb, such as bread, in a diabetes meal plan. They provide about 80 calories and 15 grams of carbohydrate per ½-cup serving—much more than non-starchy vegetables.

Non-starchy vegetables fit well into a diabetes meal plan because they don't raise your glucose as much as starchy vegetables. They also are lower in calories than starchy vegetables, making them good for dieters. But starchy vegetables still have important nutrients for health, so go ahead and eat them as long as they fit into your meal plan.

Q: How do you cook your own meals, such as spaghetti with sauce, stews, or casseroles, and figure out the amounts of calories, carbohydrates, and fats? I can determine the individual foods, but mixed dishes are very confusing.

A: The best approach is to use an online nutrition database such as the American Diabetes Association's MyFoodAdvisor at diabetes.org. This site lets you type in the ingredients in your recipe and then tells you the amount of carbohydrate, calories, saturated fat, sodium, and fiber in each serving.

If you can't find the ingredients you're looking for, visit the USDA's Nutrition Database at http://www.nal.usda.gov/fnic/food comp/search/. It has an extensive listing of foods but is a little more work to use. Just search for ingredients in your dish and jot down the calories and carbohydrate and fat grams for each item. This site doesn't compile the ingredients into a recipe, so you'll need to add up the total calories, fat, and carbohydrate and then divide by the number of servings in the dish.

Q: How can I get more omega-3 fatty acids in my diet?

A: It's great that you're trying to get more omega-3 fatty acids. Eating a diet rich in omega-3 fats—namely eicosapentaenoic acid (EPA) and docosahexaenoic acid (DHA)—is good for everyone but is especially important for people with diabetes, whose risk of heart disease is three times greater than normal. In one study from the Harvard University School of Public Health, women with type 2 diabetes who ate fish (a rich source of omega-3s) at least one to three times a month had a 40 percent lower risk of heart disease than those who ate fish less than once a month.

Although fish is a great source of omega-3s, there are other ways to get it. You can add walnuts to your diet by having them as a snack or using them as an ingredient, such as a coating on chicken or a crunchy topping on a baked crisp. You can mix ground flaxseed into yogurt or stir 2 tablespoons of ground flaxseed into muffin or pancake batters in place of the same amount of flour. You can also choose canola-based mayonnaise, margarine, and cooking spray and use omega-3 eggs when making omelets and egg dishes. Although none of these foods have the high amounts of omega-3 fats found in salmon, they are a good alternative for people who don't like fish.

Aim for 4 to 6 servings of healthful fat sources per day. Each fat serving (5 grams of fat) translates to 45 calories, for a total of 180 to 270 fat calories per day.

slow-cooked dinners

Do the prep work in the morning and dinner's ready that evening. That's what makes slow-cooker meals so popular. Here you'll find recipes for pot roast, pork chops, chili, and other slow-cooked favorites.

mushroom-sauced pork chops

17 g carb

SERVINGS 4 (4 ounces meat and about ½ cup mushroom sauce each)
PREP 20 minutes   **COOK** 8 to 9 hours (low) or 4 to 4½ hours (high)

- 4 pork loin chops, ¾ inch thick (about 1¾ pounds total)
- 1 tablespoon oil
  Nonstick cooking spray
- 1 small onion, thinly sliced
- 2 tablespoons quick-cooking tapioca
- 1 10¾-ounce can reduced-fat and reduced-sodium condensed cream of mushroom soup
- ½ cup apple juice or apple cider
- 1 teaspoon Worcestershire sauce
- 2 teaspoons snipped fresh thyme or ¾ teaspoon dried thyme, crushed
- ¼ teaspoon garlic powder
- 1½ cups sliced fresh mushrooms
  Fresh thyme sprigs (optional)

1. Trim fat from chops. In a large skillet, heat oil over medium heat. Add chops; cook until browned, turning to brown evenly. Drain off fat. Coat the inside of a 3½- or 4-quart slow cooker with nonstick cooking spray. Place onion in a 3½- or 4-quart slow cooker. Add chops. Using a mortar and pestle, crush tapioca. In a medium bowl, combine tapioca, mushroom soup, apple juice, Worcestershire sauce, thyme, and garlic powder; stir in mushrooms. Pour over chops in slow cooker.

2. Cover and cook on low-heat setting for 8 to 9 hours or on high-heat setting for 4 to 4½ hours. If desired, garnish with thyme sprigs.

TEST KITCHEN TIP: If you prefer to use a 5- to 6-quart slow cooker, use 6 pork loin chops. Leave the remaining ingredient amounts the same and prepare as directed.

NUTRITION FACTS PER SERVING: 330 cal., 10 g total fat (3 g sat. fat), 110 mg chol., 381 mg sodium, 17 g carb., 1 g fiber, 39 g pro. Exchanges: 1 other carb., 5 lean meat, .5 vegetable, .5 fat. Carb choices: 1.

Asian pork sandwiches

27 g carb

SERVINGS 8 (1 bun, ½ cup meat, ¼ cup shredded cabbage, and ¼ cup juices each)
PREP 25 minutes   **COOK** 10 to 12 hours (low) or 5½ to 6 hours (high)

- 1 2½- to 3-pound pork shoulder roast
- 1 cup apple juice or apple cider
- 2 tablespoons reduced-sodium soy sauce
- 2 tablespoons hoisin sauce
- 1½ teaspoons five-spice powder
- 8 whole wheat hamburger buns, split and toasted
- 2 cups shredded napa cabbage or packaged shredded broccoli (broccoli slaw mix)

1. Trim fat from meat. If necessary, cut roast to fit into a 3½- or 4-quart slow cooker. Place meat in cooker. In a small bowl, combine apple juice or cider, soy sauce, hoisin sauce, and five-spice powder. Pour over roast.
2. Cover; cook on low-heat setting for 10 to 12 hours or on high heat setting for 5½ to 6 hours.
3. Remove meat from cooker, reserving juices. Remove meat from bone; discard bone. Using forks, shred meat. Place ½ cup meat on each bun bottom. Top with ¼ cup shredded cabbage or broccoli; add bun tops. Skim fat from juices. Serve juices in individual serving bowls for dipping.

NUTRITION FACTS PER SERVING: 335 cal., 9 g total fat (3 g sat. fat), 92 mg chol., 513 mg sodium, 27 g carb., 2 g fiber, 33 g pro. Exchanges: 2 starch, 4 lean meat. Carb choices: 2.

pork and cider stew

33 g carb

SERVINGS 5 (1½ cups each)   **PREP** 25 minutes   **COOK** 7 to 8 hours (low) or 3½ to 4 hours (high)

1 pound boneless pork shoulder roast
2 cups peeled cubed sweet potatoes
2 medium parsnips, peeled and cut into ½-inch pieces (1¾ cups)
2 small apples, cored and cut into ¼-inch slices (1¾ cups)
1 medium onion, chopped
¾ teaspoon dried thyme, crushed
½ teaspoon dried rosemary, crushed
½ teaspoon salt
¼ teaspoon black pepper
1 cup apple cider or apple juice
1 cup reduced-sodium chicken broth

1. Trim fat from meat. Cut pork into ¾-inch cubes.
2. In a 3½- or 4-quart slow cooker, layer potatoes, parsnips, apples, and onion. Sprinkle with thyme, rosemary, salt, and pepper. Add meat. Pour apple cider or juice and broth over all.
3. Cover and cook on low-heat setting for 7 to 8 hours or on high-heat setting for 3½ to 4 hours or until meat and vegetables are tender. Ladle into bowls.

NUTRITION FACTS PER SERVING: 262 cal., 6 g total fat (2 g sat. fat), 59 mg chol., 461 mg sodium, 33 g carb., 5 g fiber, 21 g pro. Exchanges: 1 starch, 2.5 lean meat, 1 fruit. Carb choices: 2.

Cajun pot roast with sweet peppers

6 g carb

SERVINGS 8 (3 ounces meat and ⅓ cup vegetables each)   **PREP** 20 minutes
COOK 8 to 10 hours (low) or 4 to 5 hours (high)

- 1 **2- to 2½-pound boneless beef chuck pot roast**
- 1 **tablespoon salt-free Cajun seasoning**
- ½ **teaspoon bottled hot pepper sauce**
- ⅛ **teaspoon black pepper**
- 1 **14½-ounce can no-salt-added diced tomatoes, undrained**
- 3 **medium assorted sweet peppers, cut into strips**
  Black pepper (optional)

1. Trim fat from meat. Sprinkle Cajun seasoning evenly over meat; rub in with your fingers. If necessary, cut meat to fit into a 3½- or 4-quart slow cooker. Place meat in slow cooker. Add hot pepper sauce and the ⅛ teaspoon black pepper. Pour undrained tomatoes over meat in slow cooker.
2. Cover and cook on low-heat setting for 8 to 10 hours or on high-heat setting for 4 to 5 hours, adding pepper strips for the last 30 minutes of cooking.
3. Transfer meat to a cutting board. Slice meat and transfer to a serving platter. Drain vegetables, discarding cooking liquid. Serve meat with vegetables. If desired, sprinkle individual servings with black pepper.

NUTRITION FACTS PER SERVING: 174 cal., 5 g total fat (2 g sat. fat), 67 mg chol., 86 mg sodium, 6 g carb., 2 g fiber, 25 g pro. Exchanges: 3 very lean meat, 1 vegetable, 1 fat. Carb choices: .5.

hearty beef chili

32 g carb

SERVINGS 8 (1½ cups each)   **PREP** 15 minutes   **COOK** 8 to 10 hours (low) plus 15 minutes on high or 4 to 5 hours (high)

- 1 28-ounce can whole tomatoes, cut up, undrained
- 1 10-ounce can diced tomatoes and green chiles, undrained
- 2 cups low-sodium vegetable or tomato juice
- 1 to 2 tablespoons chili powder
- 1 teaspoon ground cumin
- 1 teaspoon dried oregano, crushed
- 3 cloves garlic, minced
- 1½ pounds beef stew meat, cut into 1-inch cubes
- 2 cups chopped onions
- 1½ cups chopped celery
- 1 cup chopped green sweet pepper
- 2 15- or 16-ounce cans red kidney beans, rinsed and drained
  Toppings such as shredded reduced-fat cheddar cheese, light sour cream, thinly sliced green onion, snipped fresh cilantro, thinly sliced fresh jalapeño chile peppers, and/or sliced ripe olives (optional)

1. In a 5½- or 6-quart slow cooker, combine both cans of undrained tomatoes, vegetable or tomato juice, chili powder, cumin, oregano, and garlic. Stir in the meat, onions, celery, and sweet pepper.
2. Cover and cook on low-heat setting for 8 to 10 hours or on high-heat setting for 4 to 5 hours. If using low-heat setting, turn to high-heat setting. Stir in the beans; cook for 15 minutes more. Spoon into bowls. If desired, serve with toppings.

 NUTRITION FACTS PER SERVING: 253 cal., 4 g total fat (1 g sat. fat), 50 mg chol., 590 mg sodium, 32 g carb., 9 g fiber, 28 g pro. Exchanges: 1.5 starch, 2.5 lean meat, 2 vegetable. Carb choices: 2.

southwestern steak roll-ups

23 g carb

SERVINGS 6 (1 tortilla with about 1 cup meat and vegetables each)   **PREP** 15 minutes
COOK 7 to 8 hours (low) or 3½ to 4 hours (high)

- 1½ pounds beef flank steak
- 1 16-ounce package frozen (yellow, green, and red) sweet peppers and onions stir-fry vegetables
- 1 14½-ounce can Mexican-style stewed tomatoes, undrained
- 1 small fresh jalapeño chile pepper, seeded and finely chopped* (optional)
- 2 teaspoons chili powder
- 6 6- to 7-inch regular or whole wheat flour tortillas, warmed**
   Lime wedges (optional)

1. Trim fat from steak. If necessary, cut meat to fit in cooker. Place meat in a 3½- or 4-quart slow cooker. Add frozen vegetables. In a medium bowl, stir together undrained tomatoes, jalapeño pepper (if using), and chili powder. Pour over meat in cooker.
2. Cover and cook on low-heat setting for 7 to 8 hours or on high-heat setting for 3½ to 4 hours. Remove meat from cooker; slice across the grain. Using a slotted spoon, remove vegetables from cooker. Divide meat and vegetables among warm tortillas; roll up. Serve with lime wedges, if desired.

*See tip on page 27.
**NOTE: To warm tortillas, stack tortillas and wrap tightly in aluminum foil. Heat in a 350°F oven for about 10 minutes or until heated through.

NUTRITION FACTS PER SERVING: 315 cal., 10 g total fat (2 g sat. fat), 37 mg chol., 326 mg sodium, 23 g carb., 1 g fiber, 29 g pro. Exchanges: 1 starch, 3 lean meat, 1.5 vegetable, 1 fat. Carb choices: 1.5.

Make It Lighter

Brush your teeth or chew a stick of sugar free gum immediately after meals. The minty feeling can keep you from sneaking into the refrigerator for leftovers or dessert.

Make It Fast

Skip a trip to the store if you run out of fresh garlic and use garlic powder (not garlic salt) instead. A half teaspoon of garlic powder is equivalent to one fresh clove.

fireside beef stew

15 g carb

SERVINGS 6 (1⅓ cups each) **PREP** 25 minutes **COOK** 8 to 10 hours (low) plus 15 minutes on high or 4 to 5 hours (high)

1½ pounds boneless beef chuck pot roast
1 pound butternut squash, peeled, seeded, and cut into 1-inch pieces (about 2½ cups)
2 small onions, cut into wedges
2 cloves garlic, minced
1 14-ounce can reduced-sodium beef broth
1 8-ounce can tomato sauce
2 tablespoons Worcestershire sauce
1 teaspoon dry mustard
¼ teaspoon black pepper
⅛ teaspoon ground allspice
2 tablespoons cold water
4 teaspoons cornstarch
1 9-ounce package frozen Italian green beans

1. Trim fat from meat. Cut meat into 1-inch pieces. Place meat in a 3½- to 4½-quart slow cooker. Add squash, onions, and garlic. Stir in broth, tomato sauce, Worcestershire sauce, dry mustard, pepper, and allspice.
2. Cover and cook on low-heat setting for 8 to 10 hours or on high-heat setting for 4 to 5 hours.
3. If using low-heat setting, turn to high-heat setting. In a small bowl, combine cold water and cornstarch. Stir cornstarch mixture and green beans into mixture in slow cooker. Cover and cook for about 15 minutes more or until thickened.

NUTRITION FACTS PER SERVING: 206 cal., 4 g total fat (1 g sat. fat), 67 mg chol., 440 mg sodium, 15 g carb., 3 g fiber, 27 g pro. Exchanges: .5 starch, 2.5 lean meat, 1.5 vegetable. Carb choices: 1.

sloppy joes with a kick

29 g carb

SERVINGS 8 (1 bun and ½ cup meat mixture each)   **PREP** 20 minutes
COOK 6 to 8 hours (low) or 3 to 4 hours (high)

1½	pounds lean ground beef
1	cup chopped onion
1	clove garlic, minced
1	6-ounce can vegetable juice
½	cup ketchup
½	cup water
2	tablespoons sugar or substitute equivalent to 2 tablespoons sugar*
2	tablespoons chopped, canned jalapeño chile peppers (optional)
1	tablespoon mustard
2	teaspoons chili powder
1	teaspoon Worcestershire sauce
8	whole wheat hamburger buns, split and toasted
½	cup shredded reduced-fat cheddar cheese (2 ounces; optional)

1. In a large skillet, cook ground beef, onion, and garlic until meat is brown and onion is tender. Drain off fat.
2. Meanwhile, in a 3½- or 4-quart slow cooker, combine vegetable juice, ketchup, water, sugar, jalapeño peppers (if desired), mustard, chili powder, and Worcestershire sauce. Stir in meat mixture.
3. Cover and cook on low-heat setting for 6 to 8 hours or on high-heat setting for 3 to 4 hours. Spoon about ½ cup meat mixture onto each bun bottom. If desired, sprinkle with cheese and serve with sweet pepper strips. Replace bun tops.

*SUGAR SUBSTITUTES: Choose from Splenda granular or Sweet'N Low bulk or packets. Follow package directions to use product amount equivalent to 2 tablespoons sugar.

NUTRITION FACTS PER SERVING: 294 cal., 11 g total fat (4 g sat. fat), 55 mg chol., 500 mg sodium, 29 g carb., 2 g fiber, 20 g pro. Exchanges: 2 starch, 2 medium-fat meat, .5 fat. Carb choices: 2.
PER SERVING WITH SUGAR SUBSTITUTE: same as above, except 292 calories, 29 g carb., 9 g sugar.

spinach, chicken, and wild rice soup

19 g carb

SERVINGS 6 (1½ cups each)   **PREP** 15 minutes   **COOK** 7 to 8 hours (low) or 3½ to 4 hours (high)

- 3 cups water
- 1 14-ounce can reduced-sodium chicken broth
- 1 10¾-ounce can reduced-fat and reduced-sodium condensed cream of chicken soup
- ⅔ cup uncooked wild rice, rinsed and drained
- ½ teaspoon dried thyme, crushed
- ¼ teaspoon black pepper
- 3 cups chopped cooked chicken breast or turkey breast (about 1 pound)
- 2 cups shredded fresh spinach

1. In a 3½- or 4-quart slow cooker, combine water, broth, cream of chicken soup, wild rice, thyme, and pepper.
2. Cover and cook on low-heat setting for 7 to 8 hours or on high-heat setting for 3½ to 4 hours.
3. To serve, stir in chicken and spinach until heated.

NUTRITION FACTS PER SERVING: 216 cal., 4 g total fat (1 g sat. fat), 64 mg chol., 397 mg sodium, 19 g carb., 2 g fiber, 26 g pro. Exchanges: 1 starch, 3 very lean meat, .5 vegetable, .5 fat. Carb choices: 1.

chicken fajita chili

22 g carb

SERVINGS 6 (about 1½ cups each)   **PREP** 20 minutes   **COOK** 4 to 5 hours (low) or 2 to 2½ hours (high)

- 2 pounds skinless, boneless chicken breast halves, cut into 1-inch pieces
- 1 tablespoon chili powder
- 1 teaspoon fajita seasoning
- ½ teaspoon ground cumin
- 2 cloves garlic, minced
  Nonstick cooking spray
- 2 14½-ounce cans no-salt-added diced tomatoes, undrained
- 1 16-ounce package frozen sweet peppers (yellow, green, and red) and onions stir-fry vegetables
- 1 15-ounce can cannellini beans (white kidney beans), rinsed and drained
- 3 tablespoons shredded reduced-fat cheddar cheese (optional)

1. In a medium bowl, combine chicken, chili powder, fajita seasoning, cumin, and garlic; toss to coat. Coat an unheated large skillet with nonstick cooking spray. Preheat skillet over medium-high heat. Cook chicken, half at a time, in hot skillet until browned on all sides, stirring occasionally.

2. Place chicken in a 3½- or 4-quart slow cooker. Add undrained tomatoes, frozen vegetables, and cannellini beans. Cover and cook on low-heat setting for 4 to 5 hours or on high-heat setting for 2 to 2½ hours.

3. If desired, top individual servings with shredded cheese.

NUTRITION FACTS PER SERVING: 261 cal., 2 g total fat (1 g sat. fat), 88 mg chol., 294 mg sodium, 22 g carb., 7 g fiber, 41 g pro. Exchanges: 1 starch, 4 lean meat, 1.5 vegetable. Carb choices: 1.5.

jambalaya-style chicken and shrimp

32 g carb

SERVINGS 6 (1⅓ cups chicken mixture and ⅓ cup rice each)   **PREP** 25 minutes

COOK 6 to 8 hours (low) or 3 to 4 hours (high)

1	pound skinless, boneless chicken thighs
4	ounces smoked turkey sausage
1½	cups chopped assorted sweet peppers
1	cup thinly sliced celery
1	cup chopped onion
1	14½-ounce can no-salt-added diced tomatoes, undrained
1	10-ounce can chopped tomatoes and green chile peppers, undrained
2	tablespoons quick-cooking tapioca
1	teaspoon dried basil, crushed
¼	teaspoon cayenne pepper
4	ounces frozen peeled and deveined medium shrimp, thawed
2	cups loose-pack frozen cut okra
2	cups hot cooked brown rice

1. Cut chicken into bite-size pieces. Halve sausage lengthwise and cut into ½-inch-thick slices. In a 3½- or 4-quart slow cooker, combine chicken, sausage, sweet peppers, celery, and onion. Stir in undrained diced tomatoes, undrained chopped tomatoes and green chile peppers, tapioca, basil, and cayenne pepper.
2. Cover and cook on low-heat setting for 6 to 8 hours or on high-heat setting for 3 to 4 hours.
3. If using low-heat setting, turn to high-heat setting. Stir in shrimp and okra. Cover and cook for about 30 minutes more or until shrimp are opaque. Serve with hot cooked brown rice.

NUTRITION FACTS PER SERVING: 284 cal., 6 g total fat (1 g sat. fat), 104 mg chol., 510 mg sodium, 32 g carb., 6 g fiber, 26 g pro. Exchanges: 1.5 starch, 2.5 lean meat, 1.5 vegetable. Carb choices: 2.

country captain

32 g carb

SERVINGS 6 (1 drumstick, 1 thigh, ¾ cup sauce, and ⅓ cup rice each)   **PREP** 25 minutes
COOK 5 to 6 hours (low) or 2½ to 3 hours (high)

- 1 medium sweet onion, cut into thin wedges
- 3 pounds chicken drumsticks and/or thighs, skin removed
- 1 medium green sweet pepper, cut into thin strips
- 1 medium yellow sweet pepper, cut into thin strips
- ¼ cup currants or golden raisins
- 2 cloves garlic, minced
- 1 14-ounce can diced tomatoes, undrained
- 2 tablespoons quick-cooking tapioca, crushed
- 2 to 3 teaspoons curry powder
- ½ teaspoon salt
- ½ teaspoon ground cumin
- ¼ teaspoon ground mace
- 2 cups hot cooked brown rice
- 2 tablespoons chopped green onion
- 2 tablespoons sliced almonds, toasted
   Steamed kale (optional)

1. In a 3½- or 4-quart slow cooker, place onion, chicken, sweet peppers, currants, and garlic. In a large bowl, combine undrained tomatoes, tapioca, curry powder, salt, cumin, and mace. Pour over all.
2. Cover and cook on low-heat setting for 5 to 6 hours or on high-heat setting for 2½ to 3 hours.
3. Serve chicken mixture over hot cooked rice. Sprinkle with green onion and almonds. If desired, serve with steamed kale.

NUTRITION FACTS PER SERVING: 298 cal., 6 g total fat (1 g sat. fat), 98 mg chol.,
619 mg sodium, 32 g carb., 3 g fiber, 30 g pro. Exchanges: 1.5 starch,
3.5 lean meat, 1 vegetable. Carb choices: 2.

sesame-ginger turkey wraps

20 g carb

SERVINGS 12 (1 wrap each)   **PREP** 25 minutes   **COOK** 6 to 7 hours (low) or 3 to 3½ hours (high)
STAND 5 minutes

Nonstick cooking spray
- 3 turkey thighs, skin removed (3½ to 4 pounds total)
- 1 cup bottled sesame-ginger stir-fry sauce
- ¼ cup water
- 1 16-ounce package shredded broccoli (broccoli slaw mix)
- 12 8-inch regular or whole wheat flour tortillas, warmed*
- ¾ cup sliced green onions

1. Lightly coat a 3½- or 4-quart slow cooker with nonstick cooking spray. Place turkey thighs in slow cooker. In a small bowl, stir together stir-fry sauce and water. Pour over turkey.

2. Cover and cook on low-heat setting for 6 to 7 hours or on high-heat setting for 3 to 3½ hours.

3. Remove turkey from slow cooker; cool slightly. Remove turkey from bones; discard bones. Using forks, separate turkey into shreds. Place broccoli in sauce mixture in slow cooker. Stir to coat; cover and let stand for 5 minutes. Using a slotted spoon, remove broccoli from slow cooker.

4. To assemble, spoon about ⅓ cup of the turkey on each tortilla. Top each with about ¼ cup broccoli mixture and 1 tablespoon green onions. Spoon about 2 tablespoons sauce from slow cooker on top of green onions on each tortilla. Roll up and serve immediately.

*NOTE: To warm tortillas, wrap them in white microwave-safe paper towels; microwave on high for 15 to 30 seconds or until tortillas are softened. (Or wrap tortillas in aluminum foil. Heat in a 350°F oven for 10 to 15 minutes or until warmed.)

NUTRITION FACTS PER SERVING: 207 cal., 5 g total fat (1 g sat. fat), 67 mg chol., 422 mg sodium, 20 g carb., 2 g fiber, 20 g pro. Exchanges: 1 starch, 2 lean meat, 1 vegetable. Carb choices: 1.

savory bean and spinach soup

SERVINGS 6 (1½ cups each)   **PREP** 15 minutes   **COOK** 5 to 7 hours (low) or 2½ to 3½ hours (high)

- 3½ cups water
- 1 15-ounce can tomato puree
- 1 15-ounce can small white beans or Great Northern beans, rinsed and drained
- 1 14-ounce can vegetable broth
- 2 small onions, finely chopped (⅔ cup)
- ½ cup converted rice
- 1½ teaspoons dried basil, crushed
- ¼ teaspoon black pepper
- 2 cloves garlic, minced
- 8 cups coarsely chopped fresh spinach
- 2 tablespoons finely shredded Parmesan cheese

1. In a 3½- or 4-quart slow cooker, combine water, tomato puree, drained beans, broth, onion, rice, basil, pepper, and garlic.
2. Cover and cook on low-heat setting for 5 to 7 hours or on high-heat setting for 2½ to 3½ hours.
3. Before serving, stir in spinach. Sprinkle individual servings with Parmesan cheese.

NUTRITION FACTS PER SERVING: 148 cal., 1 g total fat (0 g sat. fat), 1 mg chol., 451 mg sodium, 31 g carb., 5 g fiber, 8 g pro. Exchanges: 1.5 starch, 1.5 vegetable. Carb choices: 2.

ratatouille with lentils

SERVINGS 6 (1⅓ cups each)   **PREP** 25 minutes   **COOK** 8 to 9 hours (low) or 4 to 4½ hours (high)

37 g carb

- 1 cup lentils, rinsed and drained
- 1 eggplant (12 ounces), peeled and cubed
- 2 14½-ounce cans no-salt-added diced tomatoes, undrained
- 2 large onions, coarsely chopped
- 2 medium yellow summer squash and/or zucchini, halved lengthwise and cut into ½-inch-thick slices (about 2½ cups)
- 1 medium red sweet pepper, chopped
- ½ cup water
- 1 tablespoon Italian seasoning, crushed
- 2 cloves garlic, minced
- ½ teaspoon salt
- ¼ to ½ teaspoon black pepper

In a 3½- or 4-quart slow cooker, combine lentils, eggplant, undrained tomatoes, onions, summer squash, sweet pepper, water, Italian seasoning, garlic, salt, and black pepper. Cover and cook on low-heat setting for 8 to 9 hours or on high-heat setting for 4 to 4½ hours.

NUTRITION FACTS PER SERVING: 191 cal., 1 g total fat (0 g sat. fat), 0 mg chol., 256 mg sodium, 37 g carb., 16 g fiber, 11 g pro. Exchanges: .5 lean meat, 2 vegetable, 1.5 starch. Carb choices: 2.5.

main-dish salads

These satisfying salads are packed with
a variety of lean meats, beans, grains, and vegetables.
Many of them include homemade dressings
that are lower in calories and sugar than most
purchased dressings.

Mexican chicken salad stacks

18 g carb

SERVINGS 4 (1 chicken breast half, 1 cup lettuce, ½ orange, ¼ avocado, 1 tablespoon cheese, and scant 1 tablespoon dressing each) **START TO FINISH** 30 minutes **OVEN** Broil

4 small skinless, boneless chicken breast halves (1 to 1¼ pounds total)
1 teaspoon ground ancho chile pepper or chili powder
½ teaspoon dried oregano, crushed
½ teaspoon dried thyme, crushed
⅛ teaspoon salt
⅛ teaspoon black pepper
2 tablespoons orange juice

1 tablespoon olive oil
1 tablespoon white wine vinegar
1 teaspoon honey
4 cups shredded romaine lettuce
1 avocado, halved, pitted, peeled, and sliced
2 oranges, peeled and sectioned
¼ cup crumbled queso fresco cheese or shredded reduced-fat Monterey Jack cheese (1 ounce)

1. Place each chicken breast half between pieces of plastic wrap. Using the flat side of a meat mallet, pound chicken until about ½ inch thick. Remove plastic wrap.
2. Preheat broiler. In a small bowl, stir together chile or chili powder, oregano, thyme, salt, and pepper. Sprinkle spice mixture evenly over chicken pieces; rub in with your fingers.
3. Place chicken on the unheated rack of a broiler pan. Broil 4 to 5 inches from the heat for 6 to 8 minutes or until chicken is tender and no longer pink (170°F), turning once halfway through broiling. Slice chicken.
4. Meanwhile, in a medium bowl, whisk together the orange juice, oil, vinegar, and honey. Add lettuce; toss to coat.
5. To assemble, divide lettuce mixture among 4 dinner plates. Top with sliced chicken, avocado, and orange sections. Sprinkle with cheese.

NUTRITION FACTS PER SERVING: 306 cal., 13 g total fat (3 g sat. fat), 68 mg chol., 153 mg sodium, 18 g carb., 7 g fiber, 30 g pro. Exchanges: 4 lean meat, 1 vegetable, .5 fruit, 1.5 fat. Carb choices: 1.

superfoods salad

22 g carb

SERVINGS 4 (about 2 cups each)   **START TO FINISH** 25 minutes

⅓ cup raspberry vinegar
2 tablespoons snipped fresh mint
2 tablespoons honey
1 tablespoon canola oil
¼ teaspoon salt
4 cups fresh baby spinach leaves
2 cups chopped cooked chicken breast
2 cups fresh strawberries, hulled and sliced
½ cup fresh blueberries
¼ cup walnuts, toasted and coarsely chopped
1 ounce semisoft goat cheese, crumbled
½ teaspoon black pepper

1. For vinaigrette: In a screw-top jar, combine vinegar, mint, honey, oil, and salt. Cover and shake well.

2. In a large bowl, toss together spinach, chicken, strawberries, blueberries, walnuts, and goat cheese. Transfer to salad plates. Drizzle with vinaigrette and sprinkle with pepper.

NUTRITION FACTS PER SERVING: 303 cal., 13 g total fat (2 g sat. fat), 63 mg chol., 249 mg sodium, 22 g carb., 3 g fiber, 26 g pro. Exchanges: .5 other carb., 3.5 lean meat, 1 vegetable, .5 fruit, 1 fat. Carb choices: 1.5.

Make It Fast

Fix salads in large batches. Mix a bowlful of fresh salad
ingredients to last for two or three days, making sure the
greens and vegetables are dry. Seal the undressed salad
in an airtight container to keep it fresh and crisp.

Make It Fast

Skip making the homemade dressing in a recipe and use bottled dressing instead. Bottled dressings can be used as a marinade or dip or drizzled on raw or cooked vegetables. Just check the label and choose ones that are low in carbohydrate, fat, and sodium.

Mediterranean chicken salad

SERVINGS 6 (about 1½ cups each)　**START TO FINISH** 20 minutes

- ⅓ cup lemon juice
- 2 tablespoons snipped fresh mint
- 2 tablespoons snipped fresh basil
- 2 tablespoons olive oil
- 1 tablespoon honey
- ¼ teaspoon black pepper
- 5 cups shredded romaine lettuce
- 2 cups chopped cooked chicken breast
- 2 plum tomatoes, cut into wedges
- 1 15-ounce can garbanzo beans (chickpeas), rinsed and drained
- 2 tablespoons pitted kalamata olives, quartered (optional)
- 2 tablespoons crumbled reduced-fat feta cheese
  Whole kalamata olives (optional)

1. For dressing: In a screw-top jar, combine lemon juice, mint, basil, oil, honey, and pepper. Cover and shake well.
2. Place lettuce on a large platter. Top with chicken, tomatoes, beans, quartered olives (if using), and cheese. Drizzle with dressing. If desired, garnish individual servings with whole olives.

NUTRITION FACTS PER SERVING: 237 cal., 8 g total fat (1 g sat. fat), 41 mg chol., 292 mg sodium, 23 g carb., 5 g fiber, 20 g pro. Exchanges: 1 starch, 2 very lean meat, 1 vegetable, 1.5 fat. Carb choices: 1.5.

chicken, pear, and Parmesan salad

26 g carb

SERVINGS 4 (about 2½ cups each)   **START TO FINISH** 25 minutes

- 2 tablespoons cider vinegar or white wine vinegar
- 2 tablespoons olive or canola oil
- 1 tablespoon honey
- ¼ teaspoon salt
- ¼ teaspoon black pepper
- 5 cups torn fresh spinach leaves
- 2 cups shredded or chopped cooked chicken breast
- 2 pears, cored and cut into cubes
- ½ of a small red onion, thinly sliced
- ¼ cup dried cranberries or raisins
- 1 ounce Parmesan cheese, shaved

1. For vinaigrette: In a small screw-top jar, combine vinegar, oil, honey, salt, and pepper. Cover and shake well.

2. In a large salad bowl, combine spinach, chicken, pears, onion, and cranberries or raisins. Drizzle dressing over salad, tossing to coat evenly. Top with cheese.

EASY VERSION: Omit vinegar, oil, honey, salt, and pepper; use ⅓ cup bottled light balsamic salad dressing instead; use a 5-ounce package baby spinach leaves; use refrigerated or frozen chopped cooked chicken and preshredded Parmesan cheese.

NUTRITION FACTS PER SERVING: 306 cal., 11 g total fat (3 g sat. fat), 64 mg chol., 343 mg sodium, 26 g carb., 4 g fiber, 26 g pro. Exchanges: 3.5 lean meat, 1 vegetable, 1.5 fruit, 1 fat. Carb choices: 2.

Make It Count

Trade in iceberg lettuce for spinach or kale when making salads or topping a sandwich. Dark, leafy greens are more nutrient-rich than lighter greens.

citrus turkey-spinach salad

SERVINGS 4 (2 cups each)   **START TO FINISH** 25 minutes

22 g
carb

- 8 cups fresh baby spinach or torn fresh spinach
- 8 ounces cooked turkey, chopped or shredded
- 2 pink grapefruit, peeled and sectioned
- 2 medium oranges, peeled and sectioned
- 1 recipe Orange–Poppy Seed Dressing (see below)
- 2 tablespoons sliced almonds, toasted (optional)

1. In a large bowl, combine spinach, turkey, grapefruit sections, and orange sections.

2. Shake Orange–Poppy Seed Dressing; pour over salad. Toss gently to coat. If desired, sprinkle with almonds.

orange–poppy seed dressing: In a screw-top jar, combine ¼ cup orange juice, 2 tablespoons olive oil, 1 teaspoon honey, ½ teaspoon poppy seeds, ¼ teaspoon salt, and ¼ teaspoon dry mustard. Cover and shake well. Chill until serving time, up to 24 hours.

NUTRITION FACTS PER SERVING: 251 cal., 10 g total fat (2 g sat. fat), 43 mg chol., 233 mg sodium, 22 g carb., 4 g fiber, 20 g pro. Exchanges: 2 very lean meat, 1.5 vegetable, 1 fruit, 2 fat. Carb choices: 1.5.

turkey-broccoli salad with grapes

SERVINGS 6 (1½ cups each)   **START TO FINISH** 20 minutes

14 g carb

⅓ cup white balsamic vinegar
2 tablespoons olive oil
2 teaspoons sugar or substitute equivalent to 2 teaspoons sugar*
⅛ teaspoon salt
1 12-ounce package shredded broccoli (broccoli slaw mix)
1 pound cooked turkey breast, shredded
1½ cups seedless red grapes, halved
1 cup coarsely shredded carrot
¼ cup sliced or slivered almonds, toasted, or sunflower kernels
⅛ teaspoon black pepper

1. For vinagrette: In a screw-top jar, combine vinegar, oil, sugar, and salt. Cover and shake well.
2. In a very large bowl, combine shredded broccoli, turkey, grapes, and carrot. Add dressing; toss to coat. Serve immediately, or cover and chill for up to 24 hours. Sprinkle with almonds and pepper just before serving.

*SUGAR SUBSTITUTES: Choose from Splenda granular, Equal Spoonful or packets, or Sweet'N Low bulk or packets. Follow package directions to use product amount equivalent to 2 teaspoons sugar.

NUTRITION FACTS PER SERVING: 226 cal., 7 g total fat (1 g sat. fat), 63 mg chol., 120 mg sodium, 14 g carb., 3 g fiber, 25 g pro. Exchanges: 3 very lean meat, 1 vegetable, .5 fruit, 1.5 fat. Carb choices: 1.
PER SERVING WITH SUGAR SUBSTITUTE: same as above, except 221 cal., 13 g carb.

Make It Lighter
Toss your salad with 1 tablespoon of dressing until every lettuce leaf is coated. You'll get away with using half the usual amount of dressing.

hot Italian beef salad

6 g
carb

SERVINGS 4 (1½ cups greens and ¾ cup beef mixture each)   **START TO FINISH** 20 minutes

- 1   12-ounce beef top round steak, cut 1 inch thick
      Nonstick cooking spray
- 1   medium red or green sweet pepper, cut into bite-size strips
- ½   cup bottled fat-free Italian salad dressing
- 6   cups torn mixed salad greens
- ¼   cup finely shredded Parmesan cheese (1 ounce)
      Black pepper

1. Trim fat from steak. Thinly slice steak across grain into bite-size strips.

2. Coat an unheated large nonstick skillet with nonstick cooking spray. Preheat over medium-high heat. Add steak and sweet pepper to hot skillet. Cook and stir for 3 to 5 minutes or until steak is desired doneness and sweet pepper is crisp-tender; drain. Add dressing to skillet. Cook and stir until heated through.

3. Divide the salad greens among 4 dinner plates. Top with the beef mixture. Sprinkle with Parmesan cheese and black pepper. Serve immediately.

 NUTRITION FACTS PER SERVING: 146 cal., 4 g total fat (2 g sat. fat), 52 mg chol., 410 mg sodium, 6 g carb., 1 g fiber, 22 g pro. Exchanges: 2.5 very lean meat, 2 vegetable. Carb choices: .5.

beef salad with lemon vinaigrette

7 g carb

SERVINGS 4 (1 cup romaine, 2½ ounces sliced meat, ¼ of the red onion, ¼ cup tomatoes, 2 tablespoons feta cheese, and 2 tablespoons Lemon Vinaigrette each)

START TO FINISH 30 minutes   **OVEN** Broil

- 12 ounces boneless beef top sirloin steak, cut 1 inch thick
- ¼ teaspoon salt
- ⅛ teaspoon black pepper
- 4 cups torn romaine leaves
- ½ of a small red onion, thinly sliced and separated into rings
- 1 cup quartered cherry or grape tomatoes
- ½ cup crumbled reduced-fat feta cheese (2 ounces)
- 1 recipe Lemon Vinaigrette (see below)

1. Trim fat from steak. Sprinkle steak with salt and pepper. Place steak on the unheated rack of a broiler pan. Broil 3 to 4 inches from the heat until desired doneness, turning once halfway through broiling time. Allow 15 to 17 minutes for medium-rare doneness (145°F) or 20 to 22 minutes for medium doneness (160°F). Thinly slice steak.
2. Divide romaine among 4 dinner plates. Top with about 2½ ounces sliced meat, one-quarter of the red onion, ¼ cup tomatoes, and 2 tablespoons feta cheese. Drizzle with about 2 tablespoons Lemon Vinaigrette.

lemon vinaigrette: In a screw-top jar, combine 3 tablespoons olive oil; ½ teaspoon finely shredded lemon peel; 3 tablespoons lemon juice; 1 tablespoon snipped fresh oregano or 1 teaspoon dried oregano, crushed; 2 cloves garlic, minced; ⅛ teaspoon salt; and ⅛ teaspoon black pepper. Cover and shake well. Makes about ½ cup.

NUTRITION FACTS PER SERVING: 256 cal., 16 g total fat (4 g sat. fat), 57 mg chol., 502 mg sodium, 7 g carb., 2 g fiber, 23 g pro. Exchanges: 3 lean meat, 1.5 vegetable, 2 fat. Carb choices: .5.

Make It Count

Add lemon juice to your water or tea or use it in homemade salad dressings. One lemon has more than 100 percent of your recommended daily intake of vitamin C, a nutrient which may help increase "good" HDL cholesterol levels.

pork and pear salad

20 g carb

SERVINGS 4 (3 ounces pork and about 2 cups salad each)   **START TO FINISH** 25 minutes
OVEN Broil

½ cup buttermilk
2 tablespoons light mayonnaise
1 tablespoon frozen apple juice concentrate or frozen orange juice concentrate, thawed
1 teaspoon Dijon mustard
1 green onion, finely chopped
1 teaspoon snipped fresh sage or thyme, or ¼ teaspoon dried sage or thyme, crushed
⅛ teaspoon salt
⅛ teaspoon black pepper
2 boneless pork loin chops (about 12 ounces total), cut ¾ inch thick

2 teaspoons olive oil
2 teaspoons snipped fresh sage or thyme, or 1 teaspoon dried sage or thyme, crushed
¼ teaspoon salt
¼ teaspoon black pepper
8 cups torn mixed salad greens
2 medium pears or apples, cored and thinly sliced
¼ cup toasted walnut pieces (optional)
Fresh sage leaves (optional)

1. In a small bowl, stir together buttermilk, mayonnaise, apple or orange juice concentrate, mustard, green onion, 1 teaspoon snipped sage or ¼ teaspoon dried sage, ⅛ teaspoon salt and ⅛ teaspoon pepper. Set dressing aside.
2. Preheat broiler. Trim fat from chops. Brush chops with oil. Stir together the 2 teaspoons snipped sage or 1 teaspoon dried sage, ¼ teaspoon salt, and ¼ teaspoon black pepper. Sprinkle sage mixture evenly over all sides of chops; rub in with your fingers. Place chops on the unheated rack of a broiler pan. Broil 3 to 4 inches from the heat for 9 to 11 minutes or until done (160°F) and juices run clear, turning once halfway through broiling. Slice chops.
3. To serve, divide salad greens among 4 salad plates. Arrange the pear or apple slices and sliced pork on the greens; drizzle with dressing. If desired, sprinkle with walnuts and garnish with fresh sage leaves.

NUTRITION FACTS PER SERVING: 237 cal., 8 g total fat (2 g sat. fat), 60 mg chol., 385 mg sodium, 20 g carb., 4 g fiber, 22 g pro. Exchanges: 2.5 lean meat, 2 vegetable, .5 fruit, 1 fat. Carb choices: 1.

scallop salad with basil vinaigrette

22 g carb

SERVINGS 4 (1½ cups salad greens, about ¾ cup tomato mixture, and 2 or 3 scallops each)

START TO FINISH 25 minutes

- 1 pound fresh or frozen sea scallops
- ¼ cup snipped fresh basil
- 3 tablespoons balsamic vinegar
- 2 tablespoons lemon juice
- 2 tablespoons olive oil
- 2 teaspoons Dijon mustard
- ½ teaspoon black pepper
  Nonstick cooking spray
- 6 cups torn mixed salad greens
- 3 plum tomatoes, seeded and chopped
- 1 medium red sweet pepper, seeded and chopped
- 1 cup fresh corn kernels or frozen whole kernel corn, thawed
- ½ of a medium English cucumber, chopped
- 2 tablespoons finely shredded Parmesan cheese (optional)

1. Thaw scallops, if frozen. Rinse scallops; pat dry with paper towels. For vinaigrette: In a screw-top jar, combine basil, vinegar, lemon juice, oil, mustard, and ¼ teaspoon of the black pepper. Cover and shake well. Set aside.
2. Sprinkle scallops with the remaining ¼ teaspoon black pepper. Coat an unheated large nonstick skillet with nonstick cooking spray. Preheat over medium-high heat. Add scallops. Cook for 2 to 4 minutes or until scallops are opaque, turning once halfway through cooking.
3. Meanwhile, divide salad greens among 4 dinner plates. In a large bowl, combine tomatoes, sweet pepper, corn, and cucumber. Add half of the vinaigrette; toss to coat. Add to serving plates with greens. Add scallops to salads and brush with some of the remaining vinaigrette. Pass the remaining vinaigrette. If desired, sprinkle with Parmesan cheese.

NUTRITION FACTS PER SERVING: 256 cal., 9 g total fat (1 g sat. fat), 37 mg chol., 241 mg sodium, 22 g carb., 4 g fiber, 23 g pro. Exchanges: .5 starch, 2.5 very lean meat, 2.5 vegetable, 1.5 fat. Carb choices: 1.5.

Make It Count

Toss your salad with vegetables representing a rainbow of colors and you'll get more health-boosting antioxidants than if you used just one or two colors. Depending on your meal plan, try nonstarchy veggies such as tomatoes, radishes, and orange or yellow peppers, or starchy veggies, such as cooked chilled peas, beets, and corn.

salmon and spinach salad with flaxseed dressing

SERVINGS 4 (1½ cups each)   **START TO FINISH** 30 minutes   **OVEN** 350°F

6 g carb

- 12 ounces cooked salmon, broken into chunks*
- 3 cups fresh baby spinach
- 1 cup coarsely chopped cucumber
- ½ cup quartered red onion slices
- ¼ cup Flaxseed Dressing (see below)

In a large bowl, combine cooked salmon, spinach, cucumber, and red onion. Pour Flaxseed Dressing over salad; toss gently to coat.

*TEST KITCHEN TIP: For grilling the salmon you'll need a 1-pound fresh or frozen salmon fillet to end up with 12 ounces salmon after cooking. Thaw salmon, if frozen. Rinse and pat dry with paper towels.

flaxseed dressing: Preheat oven to 350°F. Place 1 tablespoon flaxseeds in a shallow baking pan; bake for 10 minutes. Cool. Place toasted flaxseeds in a spice grinder and pulse until ground to a fine powder. In a small bowl, whisk together ground flaxseeds, 3 tablespoons champagne vinegar or white wine vinegar, 2 tablespoons olive oil, 1 tablespoon water, 1 tablespoon finely chopped shallots or green onion, 2 teaspoons Dijon mustard, and 1 clove garlic, minced. Makes about ½ cup.

NUTRITION FACTS PER SERVING: 239 cal., 15 g total fat (3 g sat. fat), 54 mg chol., 102 mg sodium, 6 g carb., 1 g fiber, 20 g pro. Exchanges: 2.5 lean meat, 1 vegetable, 1.5 fat. Carb choices: .5.

layered southwestern salad with tortilla strips

29 g carb

SERVINGS 6 (about 2 cups each)   **START TO FINISH** 30 minutes   **OVEN** 350°F

- 2 6-inch corn tortillas
  Nonstick cooking spray
- ½ cup light sour cream
- ¼ cup snipped fresh cilantro
- 2 tablespoons fat-free milk
- 1 teaspoon olive oil
- 1 large clove garlic, minced
- ½ teaspoon chili powder
- ½ teaspoon finely shredded lime peel
- ¼ teaspoon salt
- ¼ teaspoon black pepper

- 6 cups torn romaine lettuce
- 4 plum tomatoes, chopped (2 cups)
- 1 15-ounce can black beans, rinsed and drained
- 1 cup fresh corn kernels*
- ½ cup shredded reduced-fat cheddar cheese (2 ounces)
- 1 avocado, halved, pitted, peeled, and chopped
  Snipped fresh cilantro (optional)

1. Preheat oven to 350°F. Cut tortillas into ½-inch-wide strips; place in a 15×10×1-inch baking pan. Coat tortillas lightly with nonstick cooking spray. Bake for 15 to 18 minutes or just until crisp, stirring once. Cool on a wire rack.
2. For dressing: In a small bowl, stir together sour cream, cilantro, milk, oil, garlic, chili powder, lime peel, salt, and pepper.
3. Place lettuce in a large glass serving bowl. Top with tomatoes, beans, corn, cheese, and avocado. Add dressing and sprinkle with tortilla strips. If desired, garnish with additional cilantro.

*TEST KITCHEN TIP: It isn't necessary to cook the corn. However, for a roasted flavor and softer texture, try baking it with the tortilla strips. Place the strips at one end of the baking pan and the corn at the other end.

NUTRITION FACTS PER SERVING: 227 cal., 11 g total fat (3 g sat. fat), 12 mg chol., 386 mg sodium, 29 g carb., 9 g fiber, 11 g pro. Exchanges: 1 starch, .5 lean meat, 1.5 vegetable, 2 fat. Carb choices: 2.

Make It Lighter

Choose dark beans over lighter ones and you'll get more antioxidants. If it's fiber you're looking for, any color bean will do. All beans are a good source of fiber, especially soluble fiber, the type that can help lower cholesterol.

on the side

Need a vegetable to serve with chicken?
Or maybe a slaw to go with grilled burgers?
Then check out these creative side-dish
recipes that will add both interest and flavor
to your meals.

cucumber-radish slaw

5 g carb

SERVINGS 4 (¾ cup each)   **START TO FINISH** 20 minutes

- 2 tablespoons cider vinegar
- 1 teaspoon olive oil
- ½ teaspoon sugar or substitute equivalent to ½ teaspoon sugar*
- ⅛ teaspoon salt
- ⅛ teaspoon black pepper
- ½ of a medium English cucumber, thinly sliced (2 cups)
- 1 cup radishes, trimmed and thinly sliced
- ½ of a medium red sweet pepper, seeded and thinly sliced
- 2 tablespoons finely chopped green onion

In a large bowl, whisk together vinegar, olive oil, sugar, salt, and black pepper. Add cucumber, radishes, sweet pepper, and green onions. Toss to coat. Serve immediately or cover and chill for up to 2 hours.

*SUGAR SUBSTITUTES: Choose from Splenda granular, Sweet'N Low bulk or packets, or Equal Spoonful or packets. Follow package directions to use product amount equivalent to ½ teaspoon sugar.

NUTRITION FACTS PER SERVING: 32 cal., 1 g total fat (0 g sat. fat), 0 mg chol., 87 mg sodium, 5 g carb., 1 g fiber, 1 g pro. Exchanges: 1 vegetable. Carb choices: 0.
PER SERVING WITH SUGAR SUBSTITUTE: same as above, except 30 cal., 4 g carb.

green beans with cilantro

SERVINGS 2 (¾ cup each)   **START TO FINISH** 20 minutes

    6 ounces fresh green beans, trimmed
    1 teaspoon olive oil
    1 clove garlic, minced
    ⅛ teaspoon salt
    ⅛ teaspoon black pepper
    1 tablespoon snipped fresh cilantro

1. Place a steamer basket in a large saucepan with a tight-fitting lid. Add water to just below the basket. Bring water to boiling over medium-high heat. Place beans in steamer basket. Cover; steam for 8 to 10 minutes or until beans are crisp-tender.

2. In a large nonstick skillet, heat oil. Cook garlic in hot oil over medium heat for 15 seconds, stirring constantly. Add beans, salt, and pepper. Cook for 3 minutes, tossing occasionally. Sprinkle with cilantro.

NUTRITION FACTS PER SERVING: 50 cal., 2 g total fat (0 g sat. fat), 0 mg chol., 152 mg sodium, 7 g carb., 3 g fiber, 2 g pro. Exchanges: 1.5 vegetable, .5 fat. Carb choices: .5.

couscous with orange

SERVINGS 6 (½ cup each)   **START TO FINISH** 20 minutes

1 cup reduced-sodium chicken broth
⅛ teaspoon black pepper
⅔ cup whole wheat couscous
2 green onions, chopped
1 teaspoon finely shredded orange peel
1 medium orange, peeled, sectioned, and coarsely chopped

In a medium saucepan, combine broth and pepper; bring to boiling. Stir in couscous and green onions; remove from heat. Cover and let stand for 5 minutes. Fluff couscous with a fork; gently stir in orange peel and chopped orange.

NUTRITION FACTS PER SERVING: 108 cal., 0 g total fat (0 g sat. fat), 0 mg chol., 96 mg sodium, 23 g carb., 4 g fiber, 4 g pro. Exchanges: 1.5 starch. Carb choices: 1.5.

five-minute pilaf

SERVINGS 6 (½ cup each)   **START TO FINISH** 5 minutes

17 g carb

1 8.8-ounce pouch cooked brown rice
2 cups frozen Italian-blend vegetables or frozen zucchini and yellow summer squash
¼ cup refrigerated reduced-fat basil pesto
2 tablespoons pine nuts or chopped walnuts, toasted

In a large microwave-safe bowl, combine brown rice and frozen vegetables. Cover bowl. Microwave on high (100% power) for 4 to 5 minutes or until vegetables are crisp-tender and mixture is heated through, stirring once or twice during cooking. Stir in pesto. Sprinkle with pine nuts or walnuts to serve.

NUTRITION FACTS PER SERVING: 136 cal., 6 g total fat (1 g sat. fat), 3 mg chol., 110 mg sodium, 17 g carb., 2 g dietary fiber, 4 g pro. Exchanges: 1 starch, .5 vegetable, 1 fat. Carb choices: 1.

Make It Fast

Prepare nonstarchy vegetables ahead of time so you have a quick side dish for busy nights. Steam a head of broccoli or cauliflower, then eat the cooked veggies, hot or chilled, over the next two or three days.

gingered lemony broccoli salad

8 g carb

SERVINGS 8 (½ cup each)   **PREP** 20 minutes   **CHILL** 1 to 24 hours

- 3 tablespoons light mayonnaise
- 2 tablespoons plain soy yogurt
- ¼ teaspoon finely shredded lemon peel
- 2 teaspoons lemon juice
- ¼ teaspoon grated fresh ginger
- 4 cups small broccoli and/or cauliflower florets
- ⅓ cup finely chopped red onion
- ¼ cup dried cranberries
- 3 tablespoons roasted soy nuts

In a large bowl, stir together mayonnaise, soy yogurt, lemon peel, lemon juice, and ginger. Add broccoli, red onion, and cranberries. Toss to coat. Cover and chill for 1 to 24 hours. Just before serving, sprinkle with soy nuts.

NUTRITION FACTS PER SERVING: 59 cal., 3 g total fat (0 g sat. fat), 2 mg chol., 54 mg sodium, 8 g carb., 2 g fiber, 2 g pro. Exchanges: .5 vegetable, .5 fat. Carb choices: .5.

savory pea pods and apples

SERVINGS 8 (⅔ cup each)   **START TO FINISH** 20 minutes

2   teaspoons canola oil
3   slices turkey bacon, cut crosswise into thin strips
2   medium leeks, chopped (⅔ cup)
3   tart red apples (such as Jonathan), cut into ½-inch-thick slices
4   cups fresh pea pods, ends trimmed strings removed
⅛   teaspoon salt
⅛   teaspoon black pepper

In a 12-inch skillet, heat oil over medium heat. Add turkey bacon; cook for 2 to 3 minutes or just until crisp, stirring occasionally. Add leeks and apples to bacon. Cook and stir for 3 to 4 minutes or just until apples are tender. Add pea pods. Cover and cook for 2 to 3 minutes more or until pea pods are crisp-tender. Sprinkle with the salt and pepper.

 NUTRITION FACTS PER SERVING: 78 cal., 2 g total fat (0 g sat. fat), 4 mg chol., 115 mg sodium, 11 g carb., 2 g fiber, 2 g pro. Exchanges: 1 vegetable, .5 fruit, .5 fat. Carb choices: 1.

Make It Count

Drink a 6-ounce can of tomato or vegetable juice when time is short. One can counts as a vegetable serving. (Select the low-sodium variety if you're watching your sodium intake.)

orange-asparagus salad

8 g carb

SERVINGS 2 (¾ cup each) **START TO FINISH** 20 minutes

- 8 ounces fresh asparagus spears
- 2 tablespoons orange juice
- 2 teaspoons olive oil
- ½ teaspoon Dijon mustard
- ⅛ teaspoon salt
  Pinch of black pepper
- 1 medium orange, peeled and sectioned

1. Snap off and discard woody bases from asparagus. If desired, scrape off scales. Cut stems into 2-inch-long pieces. In a covered small saucepan, cook asparagus in a small amount of boiling water for 1 minute; drain. Cool immediately in a bowl of ice water. Drain on paper towels.
2. For dressing: In a medium bowl, whisk together orange juice, oil, mustard, salt, and pepper. Add asparagus and orange sections; stir gently to coat. Serve immediately, or cover and chill for up to 6 hours.

NUTRITION FACTS PER SERVING: 74 cal., 5 g total fat (1 g sat. fat), 0 mg chol., 177 mg sodium, 8 g carb., 2 g fiber, 2 g pro. Exchanges: 1 vegetable, 1 fat. Carb choices: .5.

grapefruit-avocado salad

11 g carb

SERVINGS 6 (1 cup each)   **START TO FINISH** 15 minutes

- 4 cups fresh baby spinach
- 1 grapefruit, peeled and sectioned
- 1 small avocado, halved, pitted, peeled, and sliced
- 1 cup canned sliced beets
- 1 tablespoon sliced almonds, toasted
- 1 recipe Orange Vinaigrette (see below)

Divide spinach among 4 salad plates. Arrange grapefruit, avocado, and beets on spinach. Top with almonds. Drizzle with Orange Vinaigrette.

orange vinaigrette: In a screw-top jar, combine 1 teaspoon finely shredded orange peel, ⅓ cup orange juice, 2 teaspoons red wine vinegar, 2 teaspoons salad oil, ⅛ teaspoon salt, and pinch of black pepper. Cover and shake well.

NUTRITION FACTS PER SERVING: 106 cal., 7 g total fat (1 g sat. fat), 0 mg chol., 122 mg sodium, 11 g carb., 4 g fiber, 2 g pro. Exchanges: 1 vegetable, .5 fruit, 1 fat. Carb choices: 1.

snacks
in minutes

Instead of grabbing a bag of salty chips or high-fat crackers, make your own snacks using healthier ingredients. In just a few minutes, you'll have a nutritious snack that will satisfy those mid-afternoon munchies.

lemony avocado dip

6 g carb

SERVINGS 8 (2 tablespoons dip and ½ of a sweet pepper each)   **START TO FINISH** 15 minutes

- 1 ripe avocado, halved, pitted, and peeled
- 1 tablespoon lemon juice or lime juice
- ½ cup light sour cream
- 1 clove garlic, minced
- ⅛ teaspoon salt
- 4 medium assorted sweet peppers, seeded and cut into strips

In a medium bowl, use a fork to mash avocado with lemon juice. Stir in sour cream, garlic, and salt. Serve with sweet pepper strips.

NUTRITION FACTS PER SERVING: 61 cal., 4 g total fat (1 g sat. fat), 4 mg chol., 49 mg sodium, 6 g carb., 2 g fiber, 1 g pro. Exchanges: 1 vegetable, 1 fat. Carb choices: .5.

creamy fruit dip

11 g carb

SERVINGS 16 servings (2 tablespoons dip with ½ cup fruit each)   **START TO FINISH** 15 minutes

- 1 cup canned mandarin orange sections; cubed fresh pineapple; sliced, peeled fresh peaches; or fresh strawberries
- 1 8-ounce carton light sour cream
- 1 8-ounce package reduced-fat cream cheese (Neufchâtel)
- 1 teaspoon vanilla
- ½ teaspoon finely shredded orange peel
- 8 cups assorted fresh fruit dippers, such as strawberries, cut up pineapple, and/or apple slices

1. Place fruit in a blender or food processor. Cover and blend or process until smooth. Add sour cream, cream cheese, vanilla, and orange peel. Cover and blend or process until smooth.

2. Serve with fruit dippers.

NUTRITION FACTS PER SERVING: 93 cal., 5 g total fat (3 g sat. fat), 15 mg chol., 59 mg sodium, 11 g carb., 1 g fiber, 2 g pro. Exchanges: 1 fruit, 1 fat. Carb choices: 1.

lemony avocado dip

Make It Count

Keep a container of pepper strips, baby carrots, and broccoli florets in your refrigerator along with some low-fat dip or dressing for a quick, ready-to-eat snack.

rice cracker trail mix

rice cracker trail mix

SERVINGS 16 (⅓ cup each) **START TO FINISH** 10 minutes

- 4 **cups assorted rice crackers**
- ¾ **cup dried apricots, halved lengthwise**
- ¾ **cup lightly salted cashews**
- ¼ **cup chopped crystallized ginger and/or golden raisins**

In a medium bowl, stir together rice crackers, apricots, cashews, and ginger and/or raisins.

NUTRITION FACTS PER SERVING: 102 cal., 3 g total fat (1 g sat. fat), 0 mg chol., 78 mg sodium, 17 g carb., 1 g fiber, 2 g pro. Exchanges: 1 starch, .5 fat. Carb choices: 1.

coconut-topped bananas

SERVINGS 8 (1 banana piece each) **START TO FINISH** 20 minutes

- ⅓ **cup cornflakes, coarsely crushed**
- 2 **tablespoons unsweetened flaked coconut**
- 2 **tablespoons vanilla yogurt sweetened with sugar substitute**
- 2 **tablespoons peanut butter**
- 2 **small bananas (each about 5 ounces or 6 inches long)**

1. In a small skillet, combine crushed cornflakes and coconut; cook and stir over medium heat for 2 to 3 minutes or until coconut starts to brown. Remove from heat; set aside. In a small bowl, combine yogurt and peanut butter.
2. Slice each banana in half crosswise and then lengthwise to make 8 pieces total. Place each piece, cut side up, on a small plate. Spread peanut butter mixture atop banana pieces. Sprinkle evenly with the cornflake mixture.

NUTRITION FACTS PER SERVING: 63 cal., 2 g total fat (1 g sat. fat), 0 mg chol., 32 mg sodium, 10 g carb., 1 g fiber, 3 g pro. Exchanges: .5 other carb, .5 fat. Carb choices: .5.

Thai spinach dip

7 g carb

SERVINGS 20 (2 tablespoons dip and ½ cup vegetables each)   **PREP** 15 minutes
CHILL 2 to 24 hours

  1 cup chopped fresh spinach
  1 8-ounce carton light sour cream
  1 8-ounce carton plain low-fat yogurt
  ¼ cup snipped fresh mint
  ¼ cup finely chopped peanuts
  ¼ cup peanut butter
  1 tablespoon honey
  1 tablespoon reduced-sodium soy sauce
  1 to 2 teaspoons crushed red pepper
      Chopped peanuts (optional)
      Fresh mint leaves (optional)
 10 cups assorted raw vegetable dippers (such as baby carrots, zucchini slices, pea pods, yellow summer squash sticks, and/or red sweet pepper strips)

In a medium bowl, combine spinach, sour cream, and yogurt. Stir in snipped mint, the ¼ cup chopped peanuts, peanut butter, honey, soy sauce, and crushed red pepper. Cover and chill for at least 2 hours. If desired, garnish with additional chopped peanuts and fresh mint leaves. Serve with vegetable dippers.

NUTRITION FACTS PER SERVING: 73 cal., 4 g total fat (1 g sat. fat), 5 mg chol., 93 mg sodium, 7 g carb., 1 g fiber, 3 g pro. Exchanges: .5 vegetable, 1 fat. Carb choices: .5.

Make It Lighter

Package your snacks into single-serve portions so you won't be tempted to eat more than you intend. Or stock up on packaged 100-calorie snack packs of crackers and snack mixes.

salt-and-pepper chips

19 g carb

Olive oil nonstick cooking spray
12 wonton wrappers
¼ to ½ teaspoon black pepper
⅛ teaspoon coarse salt

1. Preheat oven to 350°F. Lightly coat a large baking sheet with nonstick cooking spray; set aside. Using a sharp knife, cut wonton wrappers in half diagonally to form 24 triangles. Arrange the triangles in a single layer on prepared baking sheet.
2. Lightly coat the tops of the wonton triangles with nonstick cooking spray. Sprinkle evenly with pepper and salt.
3. Bake for about 8 minutes or until golden. Cool completely on a wire rack.

NUTRITION FACTS PER SERVING: 94 cal., 0 g total fat (0 g sat. fat), 3 mg chol., 263 mg sodium, 19 g carb., 1 g fiber, 3 g pro. Exchanges: 1 starch. Carb choices: 1.

Make It Lighter

Drink water when you feel hungry. Sometimes hunger feelings are really dehydration. If you start craving a snack, drink a glass of water first. If you're still hungry, you'll know it isn't dehydration.

mini nacho cups

mini nacho cups

15 g carb

SERVINGS 1   **START TO FINISH** 10 minutes

- 8 baked scoop-shape tortilla chips
- 2 tablespoons refrigerated guacamole
- ¼ cup chopped cherry tomatoes
- 1 tablespoon finely shredded reduced-fat cheddar cheese
- 1 tablespoon thinly sliced green onion

Place tortilla chips on a plate. Spoon guacamole onto chips. In a small bowl, toss together tomatoes, cheddar cheese, and green onion. Sprinkle mixture over chips.

NUTRITION FACTS PER SERVING: 132 cal., 6 g total fat (2 g sat. fat), 5 mg chol., 229 mg sodium, 15 g carb., 4 g fiber, 5 g pro. Exchanges: 1 starch, 1 fat. Carb choices: 1.

inside-out tuna

6 g carb

SERVINGS 4 (3 pieces each)   **START TO FINISH** 15 minutes

- 1 3-ounce can chunk white tuna (waterpack), drained and broken into chunks
- ½ cup seedless red grapes, halved
- ¼ cup finely chopped red onion
- 2 tablespoons light mayonnaise or salad dressing
- 2 cloves garlic, minced
- ¼ teaspoon black pepper
- ⅛ teaspoon salt
- 3 large celery stalks, ends trimmed

1. In a medium bowl combine tuna, grapes, red onion, mayonnaise, garlic, black pepper, and salt.

2. To serve, cut each celery stalk crosswise into four pieces. Serve tuna mixture on celery pieces.

NUTRITION FACTS PER SERVING: 76 cal., 3 g total fat (1 g sat. fat), 12 mg chol., 237 mg sodium, 6 g carb., 1 g fiber, 6 g pro. Exchanges: .5 very lean meat, .5 vegetable, .5 fat. Carb choices: .5.

creamy peanut dip

SERVINGS 4 (2 pear wedges and 2 tablespoons sauce each)   **START TO FINISH** 10 minutes

- 2 tablespoons creamy peanut butter
- 1 tablespoon fat-free milk
- ⅓ cup frozen light whipped dessert topping, thawed
- 1 medium red or green pear or apple, cored and cut into eighths*

In a small bowl, whisk together peanut butter and milk until combined. Gently fold in whipped dessert topping, leaving some streaks of whipped topping. Serve with fruit wedges.

***TEST KITCHEN TIP:** To prevent cut fruit from browning, toss it with a little orange or lemon juice.

NUTRITION FACTS PER SERVING: 86 cal., 5 g total fat (2 g sat. fat), 0 mg chol., 39 mg sodium, 9 g carb., 2 g fiber, 2 g pro. Exchanges: .5 fruit, 1 fat. Carb choices: .5.

mocha pops

SERVINGS 15 (1 pop each)   **PREP** 10 minutes   **FREEZE** 4 hours

- 3 cups brewed coffee, chilled
- ¾ cup fat-free half-and-half
- ½ cup reduced-calorie or sugar-free chocolate-flavored syrup
- 15 3-ounce frozen pop molds or 3-ounce plastic cups
- 15 wooden craft sticks or plastic spoons (optional)

1. In a medium bowl, combine coffee and half-and-half. Whisk in chocolate syrup until well mixed.
2. Pour coffee mixture into frozen pop molds; cover. (Or pour into plastic cups. Cover cups with aluminum foil. With a sharp knife, make a slit in each of the foil tops. Insert sticks or spoons into the slits for handles.) Freeze for about 4 hours or until firm.

NUTRITION FACTS PER SERVING: 21 cal., 0 g total fat (0 g sat. fat), 1 mg chol., 28 mg sodium, 4 g carb., 0 g fiber, 0 g pro. Exchanges: 0. Carb choices: 0.

creamy peanut dip

something
sweet

Sometimes you crave a little something sweet.
From chocolate brownies to tiramisu,
these decadent yet carb-smart treats are
just what you desire.

devil's food ice cream pie

31 g carb

SERVINGS 12 (1 slice each) **PREP** 20 minutes **FREEZE** 8 hours **STAND** 10 minutes

- 1 6¾-ounce package fat-free devil's food cookie cakes (12 cookies)
- ¼ cup peanut butter
- ¼ cup hot water
- 1 cup sliced bananas
- 4 cups low-fat or light vanilla, chocolate, or desired flavor ice cream, softened*
- 3 tablespoons fat-free, sugar-free hot fudge ice cream topping

1. Coarsely chop cookies. Place cookie pieces in the bottom of an 8-inch springform pan. Whisk together peanut butter and hot water in a small bowl until smooth. Drizzle evenly over cookies.
2. Top with banana slices and carefully spoon ice cream evenly over all. Spread ice cream until smooth on top. Cover with plastic wrap and freeze for 8 hours or until firm.
3. Let stand at room temperature for 10 minutes before serving. Remove the sides of the pan; cut into 12 wedges. Drizzle fudge topping over wedges.

*NOTE: To soften ice cream, place ice cream in a large chilled mixing bowl; stir with a wooden spoon until soft, pressing ice cream against side of bowl.

NUTRITION FACTS PER SERVING: 171 cal., 4 g total fat (1 g sat. fat), 7 mg chol., 86 mg sodium, 31 g carb., 1 g fiber, 4 g pro. Exchanges: 2 other carb., .5 fat. Carb choices: 2.

tiramisu bites

22 g carb

SERVINGS 2 (3 cookies topped with cream cheese mixture each)　　**START TO FINISH** 15 minutes

1　**tablespoon hot water**
½　**teaspoon sugar***
½　**teaspoon instant espresso powder or 1 teaspoon instant coffee crystals**
¼　**cup light tub-style cream cheese, softened**
½　**cup frozen light whipped dessert topping, thawed**
6　**chocolate wafer cookies**
　　White chocolate curls and/or fresh raspberries (optional)

1. In a medium bowl, combine the water, sugar, and espresso powder; stir until sugar and espresso powder are dissolved. Add cream cheese; whisk until smooth. Fold in whipped topping.

2. Pipe or spoon cream cheese mixture atop cookies. If desired, chill for up to 4 hours. To serve, if desired, top with white chocolate curls and/or raspberries.

***SUGAR SUBSTITUTES:** Choose from Splenda granular, Equal Spoonful or packets, or Sweet'N Low bulk or packets. Follow package directions to use product amount equivalent to ½ teaspoon sugar.

NUTRITION FACTS PER SERVING: 189 cal., 9 g total fat (6 g sat. fat), 18 mg chol., 288 mg sodium, 22 g carb., 1 g fiber, 4 g pro. Exchanges: 1.5 other carb., 1.5 fat. Carb choices: 1.5.
PER SERVING WITH SUGAR SUBSTITUTE: same as above, except 186 cal., 21 g carb.

roasted mango with coconut topping

20 g
carb

SERVINGS 2 (1 custard cup each)   **PREP** 10 minutes   **BAKE** 10 minutes   **OVEN** 350°F

- 1 medium ripe mango, pitted, peeled, and cubed
- 1 tablespoon unsweetened flaked coconut
- 1 teaspoon finely shredded orange peel
- 1 teaspoon finely chopped crystallized ginger

1. Preheat oven to 350°F. Place mango cubes in two 6-ounce custard cups. For topping, combine coconut, orange peel, and crystallized ginger in a small bowl. Sprinkle topping over mango cubes.

2. Bake for about 10 minutes or just until topping begins to brown.

NUTRITION FACTS PER SERVING: 89 cal., 2 g total fat (1 g sat. fat), 0 mg chol., 14 mg sodium, 20 g carb., 2 g fiber, 1 g pro. Exchanges: 1 fruit. Carb choices: 1.

mini raspberry-chocolate tarts

19 g
carb

SERVINGS 5 servings (3 shells each)   **START TO FINISH** 15 minutes

- 1 1.9-ounce package baked miniature phyllo shells (15 shells)
- 3 ounces milk chocolate or dark chocolate, melted
- 15 fresh raspberries
- 2 tablespoons slivered almonds, toasted if desired

Place phyllo shells on a serving platter. Spoon melted chocolate into shells. Top chocolate in each shell with a raspberry and some of the almonds.

NUTRITION FACTS PER SERVING: 175 cal., 9 g total fat (4 g sat. fat), 4 mg chol., 43 mg sodium, 19 g carb., 2 g fiber, 3 g pro. Exchanges: 1 other carb., 2 fat. Carb choices: 1.

roasted mango
with coconut topping

chocolate-mint cups

11 g carb

SERVINGS 6 (1 bowl each) **PREP** 20 minutes **CHILL** 2 hours

1 4-serving-size package sugar-free instant chocolate pudding mix
2 cups fat-free milk
¼ of an 8-ounce container frozen light whipped dessert topping, thawed
⅛ to ¼ teaspoon mint extract
   Green or red food coloring (optional)

1. Prepare pudding mix according to package directions using the fat-free milk. Set aside. In a small bowl, combine dessert topping, mint extract, and, if desired, food coloring to make desired color.
2. In 6 small dessert bowls or cups, layer half the pudding, followed by dessert topping and remaining pudding. Cover and chill for 2 hours or until set.

NUTRITION FACTS PER SERVING: 73 cal., 1 g total fat (1 g sat. fat), 2 mg chol., 256 mg sodium, 11 g carb., 0 g fiber, 3 g pro. Exchanges: 1 other carb. Carb choices: 1.

almond panna cotta with blueberry sauce

25 g carb

SERVINGS 4 (1 panna cotta with 3 tablespoons sauce each)   **PREP** 30 minutes   **CHILL** 8 hours

- 1 envelope unflavored gelatin (2½ teaspoons)
- ¼ cup cold water
- 2 cups reduced-fat milk (2%)
- 4 tablespoons sugar*
- ⅛ teaspoon salt
- 4 teaspoons amaretto or several drops almond extract
- 1 cup frozen blueberries
- 2 tablespoons orange juice
- ¼ teaspoon cornstarch
- ¼ teaspoon vanilla

1. For panna cotta: In a small saucepan, sprinkle gelatin over cold water. Let stand for 3 minutes to soften; add milk. Cook and stir over medium heat until gelatin is dissolved. Stir in 3 tablespoons of the sugar and the salt. Cook and stir just until sugar is dissolved. Stir in amaretto or almond extract. Pour into four 6-ounce custard cups. Cover and chill for about 8 hours or until firm.

2. For sauce: In another small saucepan, combine blueberries, orange juice, 1 tablespoon of the sugar, and cornstarch. Cook and stir over medium heat until slightly thickened and bubbly. Cook and stir for 2 minutes more. Stir in vanilla. Transfer to a small bowl. Cover and chill until ready to serve.

3. To serve, run a thin knife around the edge of each panna cotta; unmold onto individual plates; top with sauce.

*SUGAR SUBSTITUTES: Choose from Splenda granular or Sweet'N Low bulk or packets. Follow package directions to use product amount equivalent to 4 tablespoons sugar.

NUTRITION FACTS PER SERVING: 168 cal., 3 g total fat (2 g sat. fat), 10 mg chol., 137 mg sodium, 25 g carb., 1 g fiber, 10 g pro. Exchanges: 1 other carb., .5 milk, .5 fat. Carb choices: 1.5.
PER SERVING WITH SUGAR SUBSTITUTE: same as above, except 125 cal., 14 g carb., 12 g sugar. Exchanges: .5 other carb. Carb choices: 1.

Use frozen fruit in place of fresh for fruit-base desserts. It's faster than cleaning and cutting fresh fruit and just as nutritious as fresh. Make sure to buy fruit that does not have added sugar (check the ingredients label; fruit does contain natural sugar).

Make It Lighter

Replace half the butter or oil in cake, muffin, and brownie recipes with an equal amount of applesauce or mashed bananas. You'll save about 100 calories for every tablespoon you swap.

double chocolate brownies

18 g carb

SERVINGS 16 (1 brownie each)   **PREP** 15 minutes   **BAKE** 15 minutes   **OVEN** 350°F

Nonstick cooking spray
- ¼ cup butter
- ⅔ cup granulated sugar*
- ½ cup cold water
- 1 teaspoon vanilla
- 1 cup all-purpose flour
- ¼ cup unsweetened cocoa powder
- 1 teaspoon baking powder
- ¼ cup miniature semisweet chocolate pieces
- Sifted confectioners' sugar (optional)

1. Preheat oven to 350°F. Lightly coat the bottom of an 8×8-inch baking pan with nonstick cooking spray, being careful not to coat sides of pan.
2. In a medium saucepan, melt butter; remove from heat. Stir in granulated sugar, water, and vanilla. Stir in flour, cocoa powder, and baking powder until combined. Stir in chocolate pieces. Spread batter evenly in prepared pan.
3. Bake for 15 to 20 minutes or until a toothpick inserted near the center comes out clean. Cool on a wire rack. Cut into 16 brownies. If desired, sprinkle with confectioners' sugar.

***SUGAR SUBSTITUTES:** Choose Splenda Blend for Baking. Follow package directions to use product amount equivalent to ⅔ cup sugar. Bake time will decrease to 12 to 15 minutes if using sugar substitute.

NUTRITION FACTS PER SERVING: 113 cal., 4 g total fat (2 g sat. fat), 8 mg chol., 36 mg sodium, 18 g carb., 0 g fiber, 1 g pro. Exchanges: 1 other carb., 1 fat. Carb choices: 1.
PER SERVING WITH SUGAR SUBSTITUTE: same as above, except 100 cal., 13 g carb., 6 g sugar.

peanut-apple crunch balls

9 g carb

SERVINGS 18 (1 ball each)   **PREP** 30 minutes   **STAND** 15 minutes

⅓ cup chunky peanut butter
¼ cup 68% vegetable oil spread
2 tablespoons honey
1 cup rice and wheat cereal flakes, crushed slightly
1 cup bran flakes, crushed slightly
⅓ cup finely chopped dried apples
2 tablespoons finely chopped peanuts
⅛ teaspoon apple pie spice
2 ounces white baking chocolate (with cocoa butter), chopped
¼ teaspoon vegetable shortening

1. In a medium saucepan, combine peanut butter, vegetable oil spread, and honey. Cook over low heat just until melted and nearly smooth, whisking constantly. Stir in cereals, apples, peanuts, and apple pie spice until well mixed. Divide mixture into 18 portions. Using slightly wet hands, shape portions into balls. Let stand on a waxed paper–lined baking sheet for about 15 minutes or until firm.
2. In a small saucepan, combine white chocolate and shortening; cook and stir over low heat until melted. Drizzle balls with melted white chocolate. Let stand for about 15 minutes or until white chocolate is set (if necessary, chill balls until white chocolate is firm).

NUTRITION FACTS PER SERVING: 94 cal., 6 g total fat (2 g sat. fat), 1 mg chol., 76 mg sodium, 9 g carb., 1 g fiber, 2 g pro. Exchanges: .5 other carb., 1 fat. Carb choices: .5.

rocky road parfaits

14 g carb

SERVINGS 6 (1 parfait each)   **PREP** 15 minutes   **STAND** 5 minutes

1   4 serving-size package fat-free, sugar-free, reduced-calorie chocolate or chocolate fudge instant pudding mix
2   cups fat-free milk
½   cup frozen light whipped dessert topping, thawed
¼   cup unsalted peanuts, coarsely chopped
¼   cup miniature marshmallows
    Chocolate curls (optional)

1. Prepare pudding mix according to package directions using the fat-free milk. Transfer ¾ cup of the pudding to a small bowl; fold in whipped topping until combined.
2. Divide remaining plain chocolate pudding among six 6-ounce glasses or dessert dishes. Top with whipped topping mixture. Let stand for 5 to 10 minutes or until set.
3. Sprinkle with peanuts and marshmallows just before serving. If desired, garnish with chocolate curls.

NUTRITION FACTS PER SERVING: 108 cal., 4 g total fat (1 g sat. fat), 2 mg chol., 257 mg sodium, 14 g carb., 0 g fiber, 5 g pro. Exchanges: 1 other carb., .5 fat. Carb choices: 1.

Key lime phyllo tarts

13 g carb

SERVINGS 24 (1 tart each)   **PREP** 20 minutes   **CHILL** 2 hours

- 1 14-ounce can (1¼ cups) fat-free sweetened condensed milk
- ½ teaspoon finely shredded lime peel
- ½ cup Key or Persian lime juice*
- 1 drop green and 1 drop yellow food coloring (optional)
- 24 baked miniature phyllo shells
  Frozen light whipped dessert topping, thawed (optional)
  Thin lime wedges, quartered (optional)

1. In a small bowl, gradually whisk together sweetened condensed milk, lime peel, lime juice, and (if desired) food coloring. Cover and chill for about 2 hours or until mixture mounds slightly.

2. Spoon thickened filling into phyllo shells (about 1 tablespoon per shell). If desired, top tarts with dessert topping and quartered lime wedges.

*TEST KITCHEN TIP: To get ½ cup lime juice, squeeze 10 to 12 Key limes or 4 to 6 Persian limes. Or use bottled Key lime juice.

NUTRITION FACTS PER SERVING: 70 cal., 1 g total fat (0 g sat. fat), 0 mg chol., 10 mg sodium, 13 g carb., 0 g fiber, 2 g pro. Exchanges: 1 other carb. Carb choices: 1.

cherry-apricot freeze

26 g carb

SERVINGS 12 (¾ cup each) **PREP** 20 minutes **FREEZE** 8 hours **STAND** 1 hour

1½ cups water
¼ cup sugar*
1 15-ounce can pear halves (juice pack)
1 15-ounce can unpeeled apricot halves in light syrup, rinsed, drained and chopped
½ of a 12-ounce can frozen pineapple juice concentrate, thawed (¾ cup)
¾ cup water
½ of a 10-ounce jar maraschino cherries, drained, stemmed if necessary, and halved

1. In a medium saucepan, combine 1½ cups water and sugar; bring to boiling, stirring occasionally to dissolve sugar. Boil, uncovered, for 1 minute. Remove from heat.
2. Meanwhile, drain pears, reserving juice. Chop pears. Stir chopped pears, reserved pear juice, apricots, juice concentrate, ¾ cup water, and cherries into the saucepan. Transfer mixture to a 2-quart freezer container. Cover and freeze for 8 hours or until firm, stirring occasionally to distribute fruit. Store in freezer for up to 1 month.
3. To serve, let stand at room temperature for about 1 hour. Scrape mixture into dessert dishes.

*SUGAR SUBSTITUTES: Choose from Splenda granular or Sweet'N Low bulk or packets. Follow package directions to use product amount equivalent to ¼ cup sugar.

NUTRITION FACTS PER SERVING: 101 cal., 0 g total fat (0 g sat. fat), 0 mg chol., 5 mg sodium, 26 g carb., 2 g fiber, 1 g pro. Exchanges: 1 other carb., .5 fruit. Carb choices: 2.
PER SERVING WITH SUGAR SUBSTITUTE: same as above, except 87 cal., 22 g carb., 20 g sugar. Carb choices: 1.5.

Q&A

sugar substitutes

The experts at *Diabetic Living* magazine answer common questions about health, nutrition, and meal planning.

I don't like the aftertaste of artificial sweeteners, but I'm afraid that using sugar will raise my blood sugar too much. Any advice?

A: When you want a little taste of sweetness, don't rule out sugar just because you have diabetes. Too much sugar is not the cause of diabetes, and studies have shown that sugar, honey, molasses, and other caloric sweetening ingredients do not cause blood glucose to spike any higher or faster than equal amounts of starches. The American Diabetes Association states: "Scientific evidence has shown that the use of sucrose (table sugar) as part of the meal plan does not impair blood glucose control in individuals with type 1 or type 2 diabetes." That said, sugar does provide calories and next to no nutritive value. And too many calories can lead to weight gain. For that reason, you should eat sugar in moderation and count its calories and carbohydrate as part of your total daily carbohydrate quota.

Q: What are sugar alcohols? I hear people talk about them being in food products.

A: Sugar alcohols are a group of calorie- and carbohydrate-containing sweeteners that are neither sugar nor alcohol. They include sorbitol, erythritol, and xylitol. Unlike non-nutritive artificial sweeteners, which are also used to sweeten some sugar-free foods, sugar alcohols can elevate blood glucose levels, but to a lesser degree than the same amount of other carbohydrate sources.

Sugar alcohols are metabolized incompletely by your body, so they contribute fewer calories than sugar. They are also digested slowly. One side effect of sugar alcohols is that they can have a laxative effect or cause gas, especially when eaten in excess. If you notice these side effects, check labels and see if the foods you're eating have one or more sugar alcohols. Cutting back on the amount of sugar alcohols you eat can help reduce the effects, or some people may need to eliminate them completely. Research is currently under way to determine appropriate recommendations for different sugar alcohols based on how each one affects blood glucose levels. For now, if you have questions about a particular sugar alcohol, talk to a registered dietitian or a certified diabetes educator to find out how it might fit into your daily eating plan.

Q: Which artificial sweetener is best for baking?

A: Our test kitchen experts have found that different sweeteners work best for different types of baked goods and other desserts. Sugar blends, such as Sun Crystals Granulated Blend, tend to work best for baking because they are made with some granulated sugar, which is needed to create a light and tender crumb in a cake or cookie, as well as to promote browning on top. The blends are good for recipes that call for large amounts of sugar.

Sugar substitutes that aren't blended with sugar, such as Equal Spoonful, Splenda Granular, or Splenda Brown Sugar Blend for Baking, will work fine if used in recipes that call for small amounts of sugar, such as muffins or yeast breads. They also work in desserts that don't need sugar for volume, such as fruit pies or cobblers, ice cream, and sauces. The test kitchen found that certain ingredients also affect how well an artificial sweetener works. For instance, acidic ingredients, such as citric juices, can bring out a sweetener's aftertaste, while cream cheese, chocolate, and peanut butter can help mask the aftertaste.

When using any sugar substitute, keep in mind that results won't be the same as if you used sugar. Cake volumes may be lower. Cookies may be more compact and won't spread as much during baking. Baked products will be lighter in color, and foods will tend to bake faster. Breads, cakes, and cookies made with artificial sweeteners will also dry out quickly, so serve them right away or wrap tightly when storing to retain moisture.

> When using any sugar substitute, keep in mind that results won't be the same as if you used sugar.

index

metric information

The charts on this page provide a guide for converting measurements from the U.S. customary system, which is used throughout this book, to the metric system.

Product Differences

Most of the ingredients called for in the recipes in this book are available in most countries. However, some are known by different names. Here are some common American ingredients and their possible counterparts:

- Sugar (white) is granulated, fine granulated, or castor sugar.
- Confectioners' sugar is icing sugar.
- All-purpose flour is enriched, bleached, or unbleached white household flour. When self-rising flour is used in place of all-purpose flour in a recipe that calls for leavening, omit the leavening agent (baking soda or baking powder) and salt.
- Light-colored corn syrup is golden syrup.
- Cornstarch is cornflour.
- Baking soda is bicarbonate of soda.
- Vanilla or vanilla extract is vanilla essence.
- Green, red, or yellow sweet peppers are capsicums or bell peppers.
- Golden raisins are sultanas.

Volume and Weight

The United States traditionally uses cup measures for liquid and solid ingredients. The chart, bottom right, shows the approximate imperial and metric equivalents. If you are accustomed to weighing solid ingredients, the following approximate equivalents will be helpful.

- 1 cup butter, castor sugar, or rice = 8 ounces = ½ pound = 250 grams
- 1 cup flour = 4 ounces = ¼ pound = 125 grams
- 1 cup icing sugar = 5 ounces = 150 grams

Canadian and U.S. volume for a cup measure is 8 fluid ounces (237 ml), but the standard metric equivalent is 250 ml.

1 British imperial cup is 10 fluid ounces.

In Australia, 1 tablespoon equals 20 ml, and there are 4 teaspoons in the Australian tablespoon.

Spoon measures are used for smaller amounts of ingredients. Although the size of the tablespoon varies slightly in different countries, for practical purposes and for recipes in this book, a straight substitution is all that's necessary. Measurements made using cups or spoons always should be level unless stated otherwise.

Common Weight Range Replacements

IMPERIAL/U.S.	METRIC
½ ounce	15 g
1 ounce	25 g or 30 g
4 ounces (¼ pound)	115 g or 125 g
8 ounces (½ pound)	225 g or 250 g
16 ounces (1 pound)	450 g or 500 g
1¼ pounds	625 g
1½ pounds	750 g
2 pounds or 2¼ pounds	1,000 g or 1 Kg

Oven Temperature Equivalents

FAHRENHEIT SETTING	CELSIUS SETTING*	GAS SETTING
300°F	150°C	Gas Mark 2 (very low)
325°F	160°C	Gas Mark 3 (low)
350°F	180°C	Gas Mark 4 (moderate)
375°F	190°C	Gas Mark 5 (moderate)
400°F	200°C	Gas Mark 6 (hot)
425°F	220°C	Gas Mark 7 (hot)
450°F	230°C	Gas Mark 8 (very hot)
475°F	240°C	Gas Mark 9 (very hot)
500°F	260°C	Gas Mark 10 (extremely hot)
Broil	Broil	Grill

Electric and gas ovens may be calibrated using Celsius. However, for an electric oven, increase Celsius setting 10 to 20 degrees when cooking above 160°C. For convection or forced-air ovens (gas or electric) lower the temperature setting 25°F/10°C when cooking at all heat levels.

Baking Pan Sizes

IMPERIAL/U.S.	METRIC
9×1½-inch round cake pan	22 or 23×4 cm (1.5 L)
9×1½-inch pie plate	22 or 23×4 cm (1 L)
8×8×2-inch square cake pan	20×5 cm (2 L)
9×9×2-inch square cake pan	22 or 23×4.5 cm (2.5 L)
11×7×1½-inch baking pan	28×17×4 cm (2 L)
2-quart rectangular baking pan	30×19×4.5 cm (3 L)
13×9×2-inch baking pan	34×22×4.5 cm (3.5 L)
15×10×1-inch jelly roll pan	40×25×2 cm
9×5×3-inch loaf pan	23×13×8 cm (2 L)
2-quart casserole	2 L

U.S./Standard Metric Equivalents

⅛ teaspoon = .5 ml	⅓ cup = 3 fluid ounces = 75 ml
¼ teaspoon = 1 ml	½ cup = 4 fluid ounces = 125 ml
½ teaspoon = 2 ml	⅔ cup = 5 fluid ounces = 150 ml
1 teaspoon = 5 ml	¾ cup = 6 fluid ounces = 175 ml
1 tablespoon = 15 ml	1 cup = 8 fluid ounces = 250 ml
2 tablespoons = 25 ml	2 cups = 1 pint = 500 ml
¼ cup = 2 fluid ounces = 50 ml	1 quart = 1 liter